THE GIRL BOSS EFFECT

Edited by
SANDY BEAN
and
ANGELA YARBER

TEHOM CENTER PUBLISHING

Copyright © 2024

All rights reserved.

No part of this book may be reproduced in any form or by any electronic or mechanical means, including information storage and retrieval systems, without written permission from the author, except for the use of brief quotations in a book review.

Tehom Center Publishing is a 501(c)3 nonprofit publishing feminist and queer authors, with a commitment to elevate BIPOC writers. Its face and voice is Rev. Dr. Angela Yarber.

Paperback ISBN: 979-8-9914844-8-0

eBook ISBN: 979-8-9914844-9-7

CONTENTS

Introduction Sandy Bean	7
A Critical Response Angela Yarber	21
1. THE REAL (BIG F*CKING) DEAL Angie Williams	31
2. EMPOWERED, HOPEFUL, AND SMASHING MY GOALS Allyson Mixon	39
3. A PLACE TO BELONG Stacey Halbert	45
4. THE POWER AND PURPOSE OF BEING MULTI-HYPHENATED Kamysha Martin	51
5. WATER IN THE DESERT Hailey Rank	59
6. AN UNEXPECTED TRANSFORMATION Lisa Alban	67
7. A HEALER'S PERSPECTIVE Melania Mersades	75
8. EMBRACING COLLABORATION: HOW THE GIRL BOSS EFFECT TRANSFORMED MY LIFE Lisa Ann Marone	85
9. MY PERSONAL GIRL BOSS EFFECT Kathy Houston	89
10. IGNITING MY SPARK Nyla Williams	95

11. WHY DO BUSINESS IF YOU DON'T LIKE IT?   105
    Sherri Matheney

12. FINDING MY MOJO COMMUNITY   109
    Amy June (AJ) Wiggins

13. RECLAIMING MY VOICE   115
    Grace Lager

14. THE STRENGTH OF VULNERABILITY   121
    Carmen Escobar

15. THE MAGIC OF COLLABORATION:
    UNLEASHING THE GIRL BOSS EFFECT   129
    Nicole Saunches

Conclusions in Reflection   139
Angela Yarber

A Return to the Founder: Sandy's
Conclusion   145
Sandy Bean

Acknowledgments   157

Dedicated to the Girl Bosses who fill our community.

INTRODUCTION

SANDY BEAN

I could not sleep. It was one of those nights where you drift off but you're not sure if you actually slept. Sometimes that happens to me, my thoughts will start up and my body can't quite shut them down. On this particular night, they would not let up. The difference, though, was that instead of playing some yoga nidra for sleep and pretending I was getting quality rest, I acted.

Peeling myself away from my sleeping kiddo, I curled up in my yellow Strandmon chair in the corner of my room with my phone, the illumination of the screen the only light as I opened the Facebook app.

I tap Groups

I tap the plus icon

I tap "Create a group..."

Upload cover photo?

Switching to my Canva app, I considered... what color? I quickly chose pastel pink. Purple, too? Sure. No one would really care, right?

Cover graphic created, uploaded.

Invite the five ladies I know who own businesses, figuring we could start a book club or share resources:

Search, Check...

Check,

Check,

Check,

Check.

Around 4:30 am on Thursday, January 27, 2022, in my yellow chair, I started the Facebook community that would change my life. And, it turns out, the lives of women I had not yet met, some of whom you'll meet in this very book you are reading today, dear reader.

It was an idea that had been bouncing around in my mind for the past six months or so...kind of like how someone like me thinks about getting an oil change on and off for a couple of weeks– it slips in and out of awareness and we dismiss it, then it comes back at a time where it isn't going to happen (like when you're late for a dinner date or something), so you dismiss it again, and so forth.

Does that happen to you? Yeah. I see you.

But sometimes, an idea just kind of settles into your mind and takes root. That's what happened to me with this one.

I could picture it so clearly: a networking group for women.

It sounds so dry, I get it. Why would anyone want to do that? Listen, like so many newer business owners, I wanted my business to succeed, but I did not know how to do much of anything business. And turns out, one must "business" to have a business. Who knew? I saw a few women I knew doing said "business" with some success. I wanted to get together with them. And to get them together with each other.

I wasn't always an entrepreneur. I had spent years loving my work as a successful teacher. When I moved to Florida, I only taught for a year. The state of the public schools (and, honestly, what I learned of the salary scales) along with the need for flexibility pushed me out of the classroom and onto a brand-new pathway.

I think I didn't know that I was supposed to be scared, I just optimistically let my heart guide me. Which was half correct.

I began my first business in July of 2022, stemming from a need I saw come up again and again: serving and understanding gifted and twice-exceptional children. I thought passion and experience would be enough and clients would come flocking to my brilliance (A few years and many, many business conversations later, I now know that was definitely not the case, but I applaud past me for her scrappiness). And I landed a few really great clients early on, but my knowledge of the content and craft did not balance out my lack of actual business acumen.

It was absolutely not sustainable.

Passion is awesome, but it isn't enough when you need marketing and SOPs and accounting and... well, everything else. Anyone who has started a business knows how overwhelming all of this can be, especially when you are used to being good at what you do. It can be incredibly disheartening to all of a sudden feel like you are failing.

For months, I had been soaking in as much as I could. I joined the local chapter of SCORE and worked with mentors. I read and read and read. I learned from YouTube

Gurus. I did some online courses... But the tipping point came when I went out in search of others in the same boat.

I visited a local business group (shout out, because they are active and awesome) called the Entrepreneur Social Club. It was there that I had an epiphany: these were my people! The grown up gifted kids, the theater people, the nerds, the creatives, the passionate were at every turn, sharing ideas, laughing, getting excited and giving advice in an environment that was decidedly un-stuffy. I was delighted! I got helpful feedback on my website and made a couple of friends who have been invaluable to my business journey, but I still found myself craving something more. The idea of the networking group just for women took shape shortly thereafter as a logical outcropping of my experience.

I shoved it aside.

"Who are YOU to start your own networking thing?" whispered my imposter syndrome chorus. "There are so many already."

Dismiss, dismiss, dismiss.

I knew I needed women who understood me. I felt isolated. I was newer to Florida, was buried in client work for my fledgling company, trying to figure out how to make it actually work, and momming my three neurodivergent girls. I didn't have the village I so desperately craved.

It might be helpful for me to explain that the reason I left my career and moved to Florida was to care for a child in crisis. In order to care for her, I had to heal so many things within myself (really, this is a whole other book). To parent a struggling traumatized person and not take everything personally or try to ascribe logic to their suffering is an exercise in regulation, authenticity, compassion, and love. As her illness spiraled out of control, I quickly learned that all of these things were in short supply in my body and mind. With my codependent tendencies and decidedly neglectful upbringing sprinkled with trauma, I had been walking on thin ice for a long time. A suicide attempt by your 12-year-old will wake you up to who you are REAL quick.

Once she was in treatment, and I was working with a therapist, I realized that to successfully work with her I needed to know and honor myself. This led me into examining my relationship to myself as a woman and my trust and relationships with other women. I didn't like myself. I have always had a gift for creating welcoming, inclusive spaces. I can see and feel others so well, and I genuinely enjoy supporting their success. I love people. But as for me? I couldn't ever BE successful enough to chase away my demons, it seemed. I was anxious with disordered eating and body image issues. There was so much fear.

I knew that I needed to stare that down. I couldn't carry that with me, thinking that to be a woman meant I was a mess, and that I needed someone to un-mess me.

I needed to do that myself.

And I knew that to be happy here, to support my daughters, I would need friends. I would need a community. I would need my village.

Networking with women who owned businesses seemed the perfect solution. I knew they'd likely be my people, we could learn from each other, and I could practice what I knew I needed– close connections and vulnerability in female-centered spaces. Talking about my business with women felt safer. There was none of that posturing that occurs in mixed company; no one was thinking the coffee that I considered professional held ulterior motives. No attachment or pleasing trauma popped up. Just this nice synergy. And I so very much wanted my business to succeed. It had to. With extra-needs kids, a 9-5, especially as a teacher, had become unmanageable.

So that's where I was in my head and heart when the morning of January 27 rolled around. I stank at business, I needed friends, but I was smart and social and learning to be fearless.

As I climbed back into my bed, I smiled. St Pete Girl Bosses. Yeah, it had a ring to it. My few friends would get a chuckle out of that.

Four months later, we broke a thousand members and within a year, the name would be synonymous with something wonderful.

At that one year mark, we would be hosting 6-8 meetings per month, four major events a year, dozens of workshops and smaller events, and I would win an award for the community. It is now 2024, and we are close to 8k members.

Our signature meetings are twice a week, where we connect and learn from each other. We call them "coffees" because they started with ten or so of us, in a coffee shop on Central Ave in St. Pete, long before we needed to move somewhere bigger because there weren't enough seats and it was getting a little too crowded for the fire code! These "coffees" have become a weekly staple in St Pete because women come together, share wins, laugh and learn. They have a space where they are seen and heard as they unapologetically pursue success. Bosses can show up with kids, with dogs, in yoga pants or business suits, and we are all here for each other.

My favorite part is how, after almost every coffee, at least one woman is in my inbox with a story of how this community changed their lives.

It changed mine, too.

Since devoting myself to this space full time, I have met some of the most magical women who have become some of my closest friends. This book shares some of their impactful stories. You will hear firsthand the wonder these connections have grown in the lives of real women, just like you.

I hope this book fuels your desire to connect with your sisters and support each other's success. I want YOU to have this too.

I consider myself more a conduit than anything else, and maybe that can be your role. You don't have to be all things to all people! Your care and positive energy and intention will attract members to your cause.

I truly can say that I love the St Pete Girl Bosses, each and every one. Their success is my success. And your success will be mine, too! Together, we are creating an economic and social system outside of the poison one we have been handed as women, and there is no glass ceiling above us...only sky.

Can We Talk Feminism Real Quick?

To prepare you a bit for the fire this book may light within you, I am going to dig into that which St Pete Girl Boss has evolved: women like us collaborating, mentoring, and holding space for one another in one of the greatest endeavors for economic empowerment: business ownership.

Please bear with me even if you don't consider yourself a traditional "feminist."

The idea of feminism has been a bit contorted into something at best unhelpful and at worst militant, but the heart is important. And since you are here with me, I want to talk about it with you.

Simply put, we can define feminism as feminine people holding the same options and privileges as masculine people. That they experience the same bodily autonomy, safety, opportunity access and economic security. That's the ideal in feminist theory. This clearly spills over into other areas, so true feminists believe in egalitarianism – equal access, freedom, rights, and safety for everyone, regardless of race, age, ability, gender identity, etc. Unless you have been living under a cozy rock, you are aware that we have a way to go with this, and many good people are out there fighting the good fight.

Feminism is in contrast to patriarchy, which is, by definition, "a system of society or government in which men hold the power and women are largely excluded from it." Patriarchy at its simplest is the oppression of women by men, but it also can expand to anything that seems feminine– including emotional connection and vulnerability– as being separate from the male identity (Scholars theorize that this probably stems simply from the fact that male bodies, biologically, are stronger and faster than female bodies, especially when we consider the times when we had to run away from things trying to eat us). This translates to superiority of one group over another. Let me fully acknowledge that this whole scenario is even more bleak for our sisters of color. Patriarchy is the opposite of an inclusive world, where we all contribute to a greater good. It is an oppressive system.

When has that ever worked out well? Did you read Lord of the Flies? Yeah, like that. Everyone suffers.

Society has "normalized" the suffering– think violence against women and children as well as political, bodily and economic control. Health care rights, the gender pay gap... the impact of the system is all around us, and we have accepted it as "how it is" because it is what we know (side note: this harms men, too). Eighty one percent of women have been sexually harassed in their lives, and one in five will be sexually assaulted. We are not only paid less, but expected to handle the lion's share of the mental load of households and child-rearing, as well as elderly care, simply because.

But you and I both know we are intelligent, driven, compassionate, creative, loving, living, breathing humans all our own. We have much to contribute, and together, our impact is exponentially greater.

So what do we do?

To make our way out of these situations, we need to make money. Owning businesses helps us do that on our own terms. But patriarchal systems create a barrier because they remove visibility and respect from feminine people, which makes resources, like money, far harder to come by. It is also hard for us to amass resources because of another system in which women are at a disadvantage: capitalism.

By definition, capitalism is an economic system in which resources and means of production are privately owned and prices, production, and the distribution of goods are determined mainly by competition in a free market. And, like many economical and political systems, it seems great in theory, but in practice, well...

Historically (think around the 19th century), there was a very clear division of labor, where women were assumed to, first off, be less competent overall, and second, naturally be in charge of and super good at home and caregiving tasks (which, if you've ever had a baby, you know that you felt just as clueless about taking care of it as anyone else in the room. I know I did).

Men, deemed stronger and smarter and therefore responsible for providing, worked outside that sphere of influence. And the prized roles have been doled out accordingly, resulting in the male-dominated leadership roles even today.

However, women have worked and continue to work outside of the home; so given these conditions, our options were then limited to things like nurses, teachers, nannies, domestic servants, and the like. You may recognize, to this very day, these are lower-paid and are less-respected than other kinds of careers. Women also prevail in the service industries, which are chronically underpaid. "Women's roles" are seen as less valuable. Interestingly, if you were to put a dollar amount on unpaid women's labor, it would approach 40% of the gross domestic product of our nation. So, women are literally holding up the world for free and being told we are somehow less than in terms of our contributions.

On top of that, we are penalized for maternity leaves, for leaving the workforce to care for children or elderly relatives and given little grace for breastfeeding, menstruation, or pregnancy. There is a penalty for being female. We are taught from an early age that our work is a labor of love, not one that amasses wealth. And it keeps our brilliance at bay. It makes it really hard to charge for our services or sell our products.

That's why practicing these things with other women who get it is a little bit easier, and builds our skills and confidence day by day, leading us up the ladder of success.

INTRODUCTION

Banishing the Mean Girls

We have been pitted against each other for generations. Women in ancient times had to be covertly and passively aggressive with each other to get what they needed to survive without stepping into harm's way and potentially endangering offspring. A mate. A living space. Food. Babies to carry on the genetic lines.

For so long, it appeared that there were only so many spaces at the table for us. We have been lied to and told there are limited places where we can be accepted. We have rarely been given the chance to cultivate abundant resources. It's no wonder we get scared of each other. We feel jealous. We don't want to share ourselves, our thoughts, our ideas, our audiences. We worked hard for this. There isn't enough for other women, only for us. We lean into an alpha/hustle mentality rather than an abundance mindset because if there are only so many of the thing we want, then other women are our enemies and in the way of getting it.

Scholars call all of this nonsense that attacks our self worth and makes us believe other women are out to get us "internalized sexism" and we are conditioned by it. I've seen it in classrooms, even at the 4th grade level, and certainly by middle school. Mean girls resonate for a reason. We've all probably heard or said "you can't sit with us." We've been conditioned into scarcity and disrespect.

Okay, you say. Why are you bringing this up? What does this have to do with women's groups?

The basic nature of St Pete Girl Boss is that it is a safe space where everyone belongs so that each idea and each person holds value. The "mean girl" dynamic or competition or aggression that can crop up in groups of ladies is notably absent here because that's just not how we roll. So if you, my friend, are creating spaces and connections that you hope will nurture women the ways they need to shed these antiquated systems, always start with the culture and relationships within that culture first. We, as women, need space to build relationships. Girl Boss has, with intention, given women a space where they witness our profound collective impact. It should be done the same way in anything you choose to create.

You are going to have so much fun when you gather women around you to celebrate your goals and grow together. Female-forward spaces and spaces with more diversity function more effectively. They are happier, more productive, and more creative. They are less hierarchical and more, as I mentioned in relation to feminism earlier, egalitarian. There is a space for everyone to shine, and this makes everything run more smoothly. Women are the most beautifully collaborative, creative, loving and supportive people when they come together in a place that honors the individual ingredients that are unique to each of us.

You are part of a movement by being here, looking for some guidance and inspiration around connecting to and collaborating with other women. You can challenge the status quo by being anti-racist and being pro-female. By showing up for yourself and mentoring other women. By bragging about your ladies. Girls need other girls. We heal each other in ways only folks with common experiences can do.

My imposter syndrome was right: there are lots of networking groups. But as I sat in my favorite chair that morning, I did something better than start a little networking group. I created a support community for women entrepreneurs to come as they are: with passion, brains and vulnerability. In yoga pants, with their kids or dogs, full of confidence or scared as all hell. Everyone is welcome. Because when we find each other, the magic happens– something we call "The Girl Boss Effect."

What a wonderful thing, am I right? We are learning and teaching and growing and enjoying more economic success, but we are also addressing long-standing wounds that keep us from being a full expression of ourselves.

The stories you are about to read will show you the impact of this space. Learn from them, decide what you want to put out there as you connect, create community, and witness your own Girl Boss Effect within your circle of influence.

The first story comes from my fellow editor and writer extraordinaire, Angela Yarber.

Angela is one of the women that came into my atmosphere that I immediately loved– she is brilliant, purpose-driven, creative and captivating. I am so grateful that she didn't let my impulsive name selection deter her from dialing into this community. We need her, and we need women like you, who are reading this book because you know the power of women working together towards a common goal– that is, economic empowerment. Because with the resources afforded through a successful business, we can take power back into our hands and use it for Good Things. That's what women do. And that is what I want to see.

I hope The Girl Boss Effect inspires you as much as it inspires me.

A CRITICAL RESPONSE

ANGELA YARBER

My upper lip curled into a visible sneer as I clicked the "join" button to become a member of the St. Pete Girl Boss (SPGB) Facebook group. I am *not* a girl. I'm in my mid-forties. I'm a grown woman. Lengthy footnotes nuancing gendered terms and stereotypes from the myriad academic books I'd published as a Professor of Women's, Gender, and Sexuality Studies scrolled through my mind as I conjured images of what the group's gatherings must look like.

I pictured the scene in The Wolf of Wall Street when the feds storm the offices to arrest all the corrupt stock traders and the lone woman, clad in hulking shoulder pads, cries out, "Let go of me! This is Armani!" as they grabbed her bulkily blazered arms. In my mind, there would be two types of women at these so-called Girl Boss networking meetings. The first was this 1980s stereotype: a businesswoman with perfectly quaffed hair, an expensively tailored pantsuit, and manicured nails, perfect for poking pain points as she advanced toxic bro marketing techniques with a slightly southern lilt. The second was a lithe, white yogi, decked head to toe in Lululemon with a crystal taped to her forehead to manifest abundance; she, of course, didn't acknowledge that said crystal was mined at the hands of forced child labor on a continent far away and she would try relentlessly to sell me essential oils.

My sneer transformed into an all-out grimace as I questioned the advice of my new business coach. She insisted that joining women's networking groups and connecting with other women entrepreneurs would help me feel a sense of community, empowering me to better learn the ways of business. But a businesswoman I was not. I was an academic. An author. An activist. I'd cut my teeth at protests, meeting my wife in our Ph.D. programs in Berkeley, and living in solidarity with the poor. I did not talk about money mindset or manifesting abundance. And I certainly didn't refer to myself as a "Girl Boss." Barf.

But with the exception of a few years as a professor, I'd also spent all of my life below the poverty line. With two foster children with disabilities living under our roof, my wife and I could no longer manage the constant financial stress, and the starving artist stereotype of me trying to hack it as a writer wasn't cutting it anymore. So, I invested what little I had on a business coach with shared values. She was also feminist, a queer ally, and had a Ph.D., so I trusted her wisdom, followed her advice, and joined some damn women's networking groups.

She could not have been more right. And I could not have been more wrong. Plus, my judgmental elitism was showing, revealing that my own internalized sexism had created toxic stereotypes of women that I've yet to meet in these networking communities.

It started with joining the Facebook Group, leisurely

scrolling and occasionally clicking "like" when a member posted something aimed at women's empowerment. I rolled my eyes when sister Girl Bosses talked about money, smug to rage against capitalism while bills piled high. Then something appeared on my screen that caused me to stop the scroll, raise an eyebrow of intrigue, and dig into the research I so love.

A SPGB had posted a photo of *We Should All Be Millionaires* by Rachel Rodgers, claiming that the book had transformed her life and business because it pays attention to the ways entire economic systems shift when marginalized people have access to wealth. Smiling on the cover of the book is a black woman—Rodgers—defiant in her power, owning her prosperity, and sharing the pathway to abundance with others on the margins, for the sole purpose of dismantling the broke ass systems that keep us down. I was rapt.

I researched Rodgers and her work further. Scouring every inch of her website, listening to podcast episodes back-to-back during sweltering runs along the bayou, I splurged and ordered the book, unable to wait on the public library's list any longer. I was skeptical, but my mindset was shifting. Can you be ethical and wealthy? I posed the question to my wife who is an ethicist by trade. I continued to read, noticing similar claims in the SPGB online group. I learned that entire systems shift when women and other historically marginalized people create abundance. This wasn't about having an Armani suit or utilizing bro marketing techniques. It was acknowledging that business and queer, feminist, antiracist values aren't mutually exclusive. I was convinced. And I needed to decolonize my understanding of money.

Around this same time, my own vocation as an author,

activist, and academic was finding clarity. Over a decade prior, after protests from Westboro Baptist Church, a thick stack of hate mail, and even a few death threats, I decided two institutions had become too toxic for me as a queer woman. The first was the church. Interestingly, I was its pastor. The second was the academy where I was a professor.

In the ten intervening years, I published eight award-winning books with four different publishing companies. I realized, however, that most independent publishing companies don't understand the nuances of what it means to be a feminist or queer writer; they certainly don't know how to market us. And making a living as a writer seemed out of reach.

Simultaneously, two dear friends and colleagues—who are both smart, savvy businesswomen—each spent over $40,000 (yes, you read that correctly) on a hybrid publishing company promising to help them write and publish a book, leveraging said book to build a million-dollar business. Both friends are now over $40,000 in debt and those businesses don't even exist anymore because they never made enough to cover their initial investment. That's because they signed with what I believe was a predatory publishing company. And what makes that publishing company so egregious is that they prey upon marginalized women with the promise of riches.

One of my favorite writers and ancestors is Gloria Anzaldúa, a queer Chicana feminist who claimed: "The world I create in my writing compensates for what the real world does not give me." The "real world" has given us an old-school, white, predominantly male, predatory publishing industry that, at best, doesn't understand the nuances of queer and feminist writing, and at worst, preys upon us for capital gain. I created Tehom Center Publishing to compensate for what the real world has given us. Tehom Center Publishing is a press publishing feminist and queer authors, with a commitment to elevate BIPOC writers.

It was in the nascent days of my publishing company that I first attended an in-person SPGB event. And what to my wandering woke mind was the topic for that gathering? Diversity, Equity, Inclusion, and Belonging in business. Snap. I knew then that I needed to hop off my high horse and get involved. When I let down the guard of elitist academia that made me critique literally everything and I brushed the chips of poverty induced queer activism off my shoulders, I realized that this networking group was filled with *real* women.

Women with hopes and dreams and values not so different than mine. Sure, there was the occasional designer blazer or colonized crystal here and there, but there were also community organizers, uber queers disrupting the status quo, allies intent on crafting marketing strategies that weren't predatory, and businesswomen creating systemic change in our community and world. Yes, there were a handful of white women who complained or even left when an affinity group of Black Girl Bosses was created, but mostly there were women committed to doing better and being allies and making the world a more just and equitable place. It's not perfect, but we are in it together, *comadres en la lucha,* co-mothers in the struggle.

It turned out that the reason Sandy Bean created St. Pete Girl Boss was pretty similar to the reason I created my publishing company. To compensate for what the real world had given us. In this group, I met women who not only owned cleaning and organizing businesses but transformed lives by teaching strategies for clearing out the clutter in your mind and home in order to be more mindful and grateful. I encountered women who realize that neurodiversity is a superpower rather than a weakness in business and coach clients accordingly. I was introduced to entrepreneurs who empower women to feel confident and proud through public speaking skills or fat-positive boudoir photography or trauma-informed sex therapy. Not one person has tried to sell me essential oils, but if someone did, I'd probably be delighted to buy because who doesn't love the relaxing scent of lavender?

And you'll meet some of these brilliant women in this book. Life-long entrepreneurs and brand-new business owners, women across the spectrum of backgrounds, education, race and ethnicity, sexuality, and more. Here, you'll encounter girl bosses thriving because of collaboration, rather than competition. Women living into their best selves—and best businesses—due to the transformative power of an intentional women's networking community.

Angie Williams reminds us that an inclusive women's networking community, combined with a pretty epic alter ego, can pull you from the depths of depression and help you grapple with grief, while simultaneously building your business. Stacey Halbert discusses the freedom of autonomy in entrepreneurship and how SPGB showed her that "the sky's the limit." Kamysha Martin's essay emboldens us to live unabashedly into our multi-hyphenate selves rather than limiting our entrepreneurship to one thing alone. Hailey Rank writes with vulnerability and joy about how an intentional women's networking community not only improved her business, but helped her survive her spouse's gut-wrenching time in the hospital. Lisa Alban discusses the ways mindset shifts created transformational change in her life and business. Melania Mersades talks about the power of being truly seen in a community, as a healer, as a businesswoman, as a Latina girl boss. Lisa Ann Marone writes about the all-too-familiar feeling of imposter syndrome and how a women's networking community gave her confidence and peace. Late in Life Lesbian Life Coach, Kathy Houston, reminds us that the secret sauce of a women's networking group is the safety of community.

Allyson Mixon illustrates that our ability to network has the power to shape our net worth. Nyla Williams shows how your past—even with an ACE score of 10—doesn't have to define your future, especially when you have the transformative power of collaboration with other girl bosses. Sherri Matheney's essay illustrates the power of professionalism, vulnerability, and sharing your wins in community. AJ Wiggins reminds readers that finding your community may just double your income. Grace Lager's story of transitioning from academic to entrepreneur within a women's networking community empowers you to dismantle the patriarchy one voice at a time. Carmen Escobar writes of the transformative power of community and vulnerability in creating, not simply a business, but a new world. And Nicole Saunches takes us from past and present with a vision for the future grounded in the girl boss effect.

As these essays will show you, clients, referrals, and encouragement abound, shifting my mindset in ways only the Girl Boss effect can. When I left on a 10-week Book Tour, over 80 Girl Bosses showed up to cheer me on with one crafting designer cookies featuring my book cover, another creating a massive selfie sign with a QR code to order my book, a third organizing my entire launch team, a fourth implementing a social media ad campaign, and yet another designing the website. In an affirming women's network, people show up to help you glow up. Because when one of us thrives, we all thrive.

And when my house caught on fire, SPGB was there, too. Attorneys and property managers and realtors and handyma'ams and firefighters and businesswomen who became friends, offering to pick my kids up from school or bring us meals or let my entire family crash at their house while the smoke abated. In an intentional women's networking community, it's not just your business that receives support, but your whole self.

Real talk. Since joining this women's networking group, gleaning their wisdom, reading their recommended books, and reveling in the community they created, my income has more than quintupled. Not only am I thriving financially, but I'm coaching the authors at my publishing company to thrive as we leverage their books to build their brands and businesses for the global good. Because that life I always protested for—the life where the marginalized have access to beauty and inspiration, where all their needs are met so they can thrive—I realized that I deserve such a life, too. That's the magic of the Girl Boss effect.

You, dear reader, deserve this magic, too. So, let me tell you what you're getting into with this anthology. Consider St. Pete Girl Boss a case study, a micro example of the macro, illustrating the power of an intentional women's networking community to transform, not only your business, but your life. Throughout this book, you'll read essays written by real Girl Bosses, vulnerable stories of how being a part of SPGB has shifted their business in both tangible and intangible ways. They'll also include some tips for you to consider in your own business. Surrounding each essay are some helpful statistics that provide the scientific and economic backing behind these anecdotes, along with plenty of practical advice and questions for contemplation. After these heart-felt essays, one of our amazing editors and the founder of St. Pete Girl Boss, the effervescent Sandy Bean, will guide you in how you can create a similar women's networking community. Because in the immortal words of Lizzo, "If I'm shining everybody's gonna shine."

The Girl Boss Effect is designed to share how we've shined so that you, too, can shine. From Girl Boss essays to statistics, practical tips to business wisdom, may this community of women entrepreneurs embolden you to create a better world with your business. May you, too, experience the power of the Girl Boss effect.

ONE
THE REAL (BIG F*CKING) DEAL

ANGIE WILLIAMS

"I found a reason to get out of bed on Friday mornings. I found a way to uplift people and add some light to their day."

I'M NOT A MORNING PERSON. IF I HAD IT MY WAY, I'D prefer to not have to communicate with other humans before 10am. So to hear over one hundred voices through glass double doors at 8:30 in the morning on Friday gave me considerable pause to turn around, get in my car and go home. Instead, I put on my big girl pants, walked in and afterwards, nothing was the same.

January 2023 was when I took my leap of faith on that fateful Friday morning. But to understand the full scope of my Girl Boss story we have to go back to 2022. I'd planned to move to St. Pete in February 2022 from San Francisco. On February 4, 2022, the night that I was supposed to fly out, meet my landlord and get my keys, my mom suffered a massive brain hemorrhage. Unfortunately, she passed away on April 7, 2022, setting off a chain of events that is still being unraveled as I write these very words.

If you've ever lost a loved one, you know that grief can be devastating, paralyzing and all encompassing. The other side of loss is that it can bring out the worst in people. After dealing with the fallout from my mom's passing, I finally made my move to St. Pete in October 2022. While I did feel a breath of fresh air, I mostly felt lost. When my mom died, the Angie that I'd previously known died with her and this new version of me was overcome without my mom there as a compass. I spent the remainder of the year in deep depression and barely able to get out of bed.

At some point, I looked in the mirror and reminded myself that the reason I felt lonely was because I moved without the "traditional" anchors: family, work, school, a relationship. With that frame of reference, I knew I needed to meet people that had similar hobbies or interests and build community that way. At the top of my list of interests? Entrepreneurship.

Enter St. Pete Girl Boss.

Coming from the land of Silicon Valley, most networking events are typically full of posturing founders, venture capitalists and ecosystem builders. There are genuine down to earth people but it felt artificial to put it nicely.

Girl Boss was nothing like that. I remember walking in and Sandy was there at the welcome table with her signature giant smile and was incredibly warm and welcoming. It's truly the best way to enter a room, especially when you're the new kid in the room and trying to wake up.

Admittedly, it's intimidating: seeing groups of women

walk in and immediately know each other and feeling like an outsider. What struck me, was how many people pulled you in, and included you in the conversations.

When the meeting started, Sandy asked how many Girl Bosses had collaborated with other Girl Bosses in the past week. Half the group raised their hands. She asked how many had interacted with each other on the Facebook group and almost the entire room raised their hands. I sat quietly and thought, *this is either a cult or the real deal.*

I left the meeting feeling something I hadn't felt in almost a year: alive. I was buzzing around for the rest of the day and into the weekend. I had things I wanted to do suddenly, tons of business ideas and I knew that I needed to go back.

The thing about Girl Boss is that it's something like a drug. The first hit is like something you've never felt before but the second and third time you realize you need to learn how to calibrate it for your situation. The names and faces take time to settle and you find the people you connect with on a deeper level. Freed from the mask I had to wear to "fit in" networking in California, I searched for myself.

I came in working on a personal project to launch an online course for ambitious entrepreneurs after having had my own startup and worked for a national organization that supported thousands of entrepreneurs every year. Although I felt no desire to start another business, I felt called to pursue supporting the mental health of entrepreneurs and aspiring entrepreneurs who were chasing their dreams.

While I sorted that out, an opportunity presented itself inside of the Girl Boss ecosystem: being a co-lead for Black Girl Boss, a sister organization to St. Pete Girl Boss that would aim to uplift and support the unique challenges faced by Black women entrepreneurs. I suppose that's what happens when I talk about your old life and mention that I ran a local chapter for Black Women Talk Tech. When faced with saying yes or no, I recall thinking: *Your past always recreates itself no matter where you go.*

And off we went: Mo Fields, the founder of Black Girl Boss, myself and Miranda McDaniel as her co-leads. The move into leadership for BGB also meant more visibility inside of the main Girl Boss group: as speakers, as facilitators, running segments in the standard agenda, etc. One of the segments that always stood out to me was the Wins. Simply put, people raise their hand and share a personal or professional win and people politely clap. I always felt that we could do more but it didn't feel as if it was my place to change the standard.

Until one day, I was handed the mic to run the segment and just like that first Friday coffee, nothing was the same. The win segment transformed to having a call-and-response element, a theme song and I got to live out a childhood dream to be a game show host and I morphed myself in my alter ego "Barbara Barker."

Admittedly, all of these opportunities and connections I was making were incredible but viewing things at the surface level never tells the whole story. I mentioned that grief has no bounds and that the fallout from losing someone brings out the worst in people. While I was living my best life in Florida, my former life in California tormented me and broke me down, mentally and financially. I once again found myself wearing a mask through everything. My light dimmed to the point that I barely got out of bed for several days at a time. I'm forever grateful for the Girl Bosses that stood by me through the good, the bad and the times I was very, very ugly.

In the year that has passed since my light dimming, I had to pull myself up by the bootstraps as they say, hustle to make life work and make extremely tough choices along the way. As much as I love working for myself, I had to come to terms with the fact that the stress of entrepreneurship was a toxic match for the stress that life was putting me through. I put my business ideas aside and took a remote advisory role that has turned into a full time job that is surprisingly fulfilling.

As much as I love building community, it drained me more than it gave me life. Mo and Miranda were the two best people to launch Black Girl Boss with but the most important part of being a leader is to know when you're in the way. My personal responsibilities and my desires were no longer one hundred percent in and I believed that both they and the organization deserve better than that. They were both extremely supportive in my decision and the transition and in turn my support for them and the group is unwavering.

As for Barbara? Truth be told, I'd planned to step away from her too. I went to a Friday coffee, after not attending for a few weeks with the full intention to shut it down. There were so many new faces that everywhere I turned, a regular would point towards me and tell a new person "just wait for the wins." How could I say no?

I came to Girl Boss with a singular focus for myself: get out of the bed along with a singular focus for business: help other entrepreneurs balance their ambition with their everyday lives to improve their mental health. Ironically, I found Barbara instead. I found a reason to get out of bed on Friday mornings. I found a way to uplift people and add some light to their day. Most importantly, I found out that all of the things that make me who I am didn't die with my mom. I still have some spark left in me.

As Barbara would say: That's a BFD! BIG FUCKING DEEEEEAAALLLLL!!!

Angelic Williams *is a serial entrepreneur and currently Chief Product Officer at eeva.*
www.evaa.ai

American women earn 82 cents for every dollar earned by a white man.

Black women, 69 cents.

59 cents for Indigenous women.

And only 57 cents for Latina/Hispanic women.

TWO
EMPOWERED, HOPEFUL, AND SMASHING MY GOALS

ALLYSON MIXON

"My ability to network now has the power to shape my net worth."

I BOUGHT A USED COMPUTER THAT CHANGED MY LIFE. I know it sounds cliche but hear me out. I'm actually clicking away at the keyboard of that very computer to write this epic tale for you. Are you ready?

If you know me at all you know I love to plan! If you don't know me yet, I am Allyson. Embrace this story as a warm welcome into my world and know I map out my route in life. No better way to spend time together than an adventure. I'll lead the way!

Let me take you to the city my husband and I handpicked for our family to relocate to. We had a long list of things we wanted in a city and a 5-year plan to put in motion once we found it. For years I've dreamt of building community with those that have the desire for a conscious collective to move towards decolonization. What a delight to have found all of that in St. Petersburg, Florida. Not only does this vibrant city have a melting pot of folks, it is a hub for entrepreneurs and small businesses. This is great news for me as I decided to launch my cleaning business in a new state. I had the cleaning and sales down from years of operating in Tennessee. However, starting from scratch meant I needed to meet people and establish community. So off I went to Facebook to check the local networking groups and join them all.

In the mix was St. Pete Girl Bosses. It was just shy of 2,000 women at the time. It had its own vibe and the energy was fresh. Regardless, I still approached that group with so much caution. I lurked in there for months and even more time passed before I actually made it to a meeting in person. And even then, only because I saw Denise Marsh was going to be on the panel.

We should pause here for a second. There would be nothing to read here today without Denise selling me the computer that rocked my entire world in the best way possible. One Monday in July of 2023 she added a comment to a Match Monday post in SPGB to sell her computer. I immediately reached out to her and justified the purchase to my husband. A few days later my family packed in the car for a 2 hour drive to pick up the computer. After the exchange Denise asked if I had been to a coffee meeting yet. When I told her no, she extended reassurance that I was indeed welcome to join them when my schedule allowed.

Even with her warm invitation I didn't show up to a meeting until October. As I mentioned before, seeing Denise on the panel had my attention. The coffee location was 5 minutes from my house and I knew Denise was going to be

EMPOWERED, HOPEFUL, AND SMASHING MY GOALS

driving an hour just to get there. If she could invest 2 hours of drive time then I could show up and listen to what she had to say.

Now before I take us into that first meeting can I get a show of hands for those that also tread lightly around a new group of women? [Hand raised high] We are in this together! But why are we like this?

The short answer is we are conditioned to move in the world from the patriarchal lens. Power over people is the fuel that keeps the system in check. If you're like me, that no longer feels right for my life. I want to be in control of myself and allow others to have the same freedom. I want a collaborative approach to community for the collective to rise as a whole. Wouldn't it be grand to live in such a place?

Ready to have your mind blown? Not only is it possible, it's in motion. This community exists!

When I arrived at that meeting, there they were.

The dreamers that were doing the work to create their own ecosystem. One that allowed the collective to rise. Built on respect and inclusion allowing the girl boss effect to run rampant through the community they built. These women are aware of their power and they will shine a light on yours for you and others to see, too. To be seen as an expert for all that you've gathered in your beautiful brain over the years, just as you are. I may have entered the meeting scared, but I left empowered and hopeful. The in-person vibe matched the online presentation of the group. This was the real deal and I was hooked!

It has been almost a year since my first meeting and well over a year of ownership of this fine computer. In that time my business exploded with girl boss after girl boss on my schedule. Proving my ability to network now has the power to shape my net worth. Through collaborations and fully embracing the girl boss effect I've also been smashing my own goals at a rapid rate.

Since January of 2024 I have

- Taken part in a panel of girl bosses for a webinar on religious trauma.
- I've utilized coaches and consultants from the group to assist me in sharing home synergy work with the world.
- I joined the Uplevel so I could fully utilize the girl boss effect as a two-way street with the most active bosses.
- I've had speaking gigs within the SPGB community and beyond.
- I made a podcast for others to create their own peace phase in life.
- Last, but not least, I've rediscovered that I am a writer. This very essay has allowed me to recognize that and put it into motion. I have big plans for me and this computer.

As entrepreneurs we think outside of the box as we navigate the world through a lens of our own values. As girl bosses we've taken it a step further and created a movement. Working together we can go farther, faster. Have a need? There is a Girl Boss for that.

Allyson Mixon *is a tenacious entrepreneur shaping her dreams into a decolonized reality. She inspires others to create their own path in life through home synergy work.*

Only 10% of the world's millionaires are women.
Less than 1% are women of color.

Question for Contemplation:
What structures and systems provide barriers for you achieving wealth?

Pro Tip:
Surround yourself with other women who are doing well financially.

Create what Rachel Rodgers calls "Your Million Dollar Squad."

THREE
A PLACE TO BELONG

STACEY HALBERT

"I wanted full autonomy. I wanted to help people directly. I wanted to reap the rewards of owning my own business. I wanted to work fully remotely so I could be anywhere."

PICTURE THIS: A BLONDE WOMAN IN HER 40S STEPPING into a room of older women, feeling as if I stepped into the wrong room. My hands got clammy, and my heart was racing and I began searching for all the exits. I was the youngest person in the room and felt completely out of place. This was one of my first experiences at a women's networking event. Their focus wasn't really on building networks per se but was more focused on philanthropic efforts. That is great, but not what I was looking for. I checked on several BNI groups in the area but felt there was too much of a commitment and it felt frigid. I was a new business looking for support, education, and connection with others like me. One of the women I did meet at a BNI meeting suggested I check out St Pete Girl Boss. I had not heard of this group, so I was intrigued, and of course, I got online and checked it out.

Fast forward to November 2022, I drove to St Petersburg City Theater to attend a St Pete Girl Boss Friday Coffee for the first time. I was quickly approached by a super-friendly gal who put me right at ease. She took the time to learn about me and introduced me to others in the room. This was awesome. The founder of the group was approachable and did not exude a higher-than-thou aura about her. In other groups, the leadership team was unapproachable. During the meeting, there were introductions around the room and I felt like I belonged here with so many women in a similar position.

My Why

This question can be a tough one to answer for some but for me, it came easy. For many years I have worked for others and poured my heart and all my energy into their businesses without the rewards of owning them. One day after having a particularly rough day at the office, frustrated with how things were run, my husband jokingly said, "You want your own business, don't you," I instantly spouted out "No way." Little did I know that was the seed that began my journey into entrepreneurship.

Once I decided it was time for me to move on from where I was working, I began researching what I wanted to do next. I could continue in middle management, which I felt was a dead end, or venture into something completely new. I opted for something new and began researching what I could do that would impact someone's life directly. I wanted full autonomy and control over who I did work for and what I would do.

My Thought Process:

- I wanted full autonomy
- I wanted to help people directly
- I wanted to reap the rewards of owning my own business
- I wanted to work fully remotely so I could be anywhere working
- I wanted to do something different and use my work experience and education and learn more.
- I didn't want to sell products or have an e-shop
- I wanted a service-based business
- I wanted a challenge and to do something that would be a stretch for me
- Small business - beginning/startup companies need help with bookkeeping and understanding how that will help or hurt their business. I have found that this demographic is the most under-served as most accountants and CPAs are outside of the budget.

I started my business with the help of an online course, a good ole college effort, and by the seat of my pants. The accounting /bookkeeping industry would be a great fit for what I wanted to do and felt pretty darn sure of it, so Two Cats Bookkeeping, LLC was born. I began making the space in my world for this new business venture. When I felt it was time to move on from corporate and give bookkeeping a go, I went to work with an accountant. During this time I honed my skills and started to venture out to find my own clients to work in the evenings and weekends. As time went on, I reduced my time to part-time with the accountant, began working part-time on my own business, and began networking and finding clients.

As my networking efforts began paying off, I obtained my first St Pete Girl Boss (SPGB) client and then Two Cats Bookkeeping started to get more referrals from other St Pete Girl Bosses. The know, like, trust, and refer concept is no joke with women. They want to get to know and like you before doing business with you. So the more I attended SPGB events, the more meaningful connections I made. One of the first gals I met was in the health insurance realm and was always super friendly and happy to connect me to others. Another great connection was with a Human Design guru who helped me understand more about myself and how it relates to my business. The mobile notary gal was super connected and always introduced me to everyone. I even began working with her as I am also a Notary Public.

Before St Pete Girl Boss, I bounced between networking meetings to find a place where I fit in, as so many groups were too stuffy or overly structured with very little education for newer small businesses. My business was just starting and I had 1 client and was looking to gain exposure to potential clients. I knew a bit about how to run a small business from being a director of operations for 8 years but I was eager to learn more.

After joining SPGB, my mindset became "The sky's the limit!" I now have a wealth of knowledgeable people at my fingertips and at each meeting, there is something that you can use personally or professionally. I feel inspired and jazzed after each meeting I attend.

Words of wisdom to women looking to start a business,

just starting with your business, or women who want to connect with like-minded women is that St Pete Girl Boss is the place to be. The Girl Boss Effect can be connecting with businesses to help you, learning from other fabulous ladies, or gaining friendships with those who understand you. If there is nothing like this in your area, it is not difficult to create one yourself. I am sure there are others, just like you looking for the same thing.

Stacey Halbert *owns Two Cats Bookkeeping which serves small service-based businesses.*
www.twocatsbookkeeping.com

Women did not have the legal right to open a business without a male signature until 1988 in the United States.

Question for Contemplation:
When have you done something completely on your own when society expected you to have a man helping or doing it for you?

Pro Tip:
Harness the power of a virtual community!

When you have a problem that seems like only a man can fix, ask your women's networking community for help. Whether it's changing a tire, regrouting your kitchen, balancing your business books, or filing your taxes, you don't have to have a man's help to make it happen. Find a badass woman's tutorial on YouTube or ask a friend for help.

FOUR

THE POWER AND PURPOSE OF BEING MULTI-HYPHENATED

KAMYSHA MARTIN

"Unapologetically Pro Black. Unapologetically Multi-Hyphenated. Unapologetically Fearless."

I AM UNAPOLOGETIC IN MANY ASPECTS OF MY LIFE. Unapologetically Pro Black. Unapologetically Multi-Hyphenated (more on that later). Unapologetically Fearless. And I unapologetically decided to move to St Pete after the chaos of Covid-19 made me feel I wasn't grown enough to move out of the country and be *that* far away from my family. I don't want to confuse unapologetic with easy. Because the two are not synonymous. In fact, being unapologetic can be quite the opposite...it can be downright challenging.

In 2014 I unapologetically fired my corporate job to run my jewelry business full-time. As a self-taught Metalsmith I spent years building my jewelry business. Creating is a necessity...it is not an option for me. I often say I find myself and lose myself in my studio. It helps keep me sane; that's necessary not only for me, but for those around me. And (not "but") when I moved to St Pete I knew something inside me was changing. I knew something new was trying to be born and I needed to make room for it. A spiritual transformation was coming...whether I wanted it to...or not. And I welcomed it. Whatever it was.

I've always known we are connected. You and I. All of us. "You" do well... "I" do well... "We" do well. I know this to be true. I've always been a natural motivator. Don't tell me you want to do something! You say you want to write a book...start a business...run a marathon... I'm going to push, pull, encourage, support, motivate, inspire, cheer, text, call, show up, and remind you about That Thing. Whatever it takes to get you across the finish line. I knew this was part of my transformation...helping others with theirs. Helping them accomplish their big bodacious goals. The thought of me being "on purpose" AND helping people change their lives AND creating income...thrilled me. I decided to leverage all my years in executive leadership and non-profit administration and project management into Goal Coaching. So I started SistahPush. And (not "but") I still had my jewelry business. Now how's this going to work?

I struggled to figure out how to balance my two businesses. St Pete was a new page and because people didn't know me and my jewelry I led with SistahPush and only whispered "metalsmith" when introducing myself because I wanted my goal coaching to be in the forefront. I'm really good at compartmentalizing, but this just wasn't feeling right to me. I felt like I was abandoning a business I had grown for so many years. A business that gave me life. By this time in SPGB, I was already a speaker and conducting workshops and sitting on panels and had really grown my coaching clientele. I was proudly and boldly SAYING I was multi-hyphenated but I didn't feel like I was BEING multi-hyphenated. If that makes any sense. Every time I put on my "SistahPush Pink" outfit (believe me...it's a thing) and added my jewelry (MY jewelry) I felt like I was treating my jewelry business like a side piece. It felt wrong. I wasn't giving it the love it deserved.

Around this time, I had an opportunity to attend an event on behalf of SPGB. When I walked into the building I immediately met someone who would come to change my artistic life forever. After learning I was a Metalsmith this artist and singer said... "Oh you gotta make me something special." I had no idea how special it would be. After several months we eventually met and she commissioned me to make a metal brassiere for a big show she had coming up. She also wanted a metal headpiece...and a necklace...and ring. I said, "of course," at least that's what I said aloud. Inside I admonished myself with some self-talk, "What are you saying? You've never made a metal bra before! What the hell are you saying yes for?" Talk about being pushed outside my comfort zone.

I had 4 weeks to make these pieces. Then, I got very sick. I was totally down for 2 weeks. I had 2 weeks to make something I had never made before. I needed all the stars to align on this one. Two days before the show, she decided she didn't want to wear shoes...so she requested foot jewelry. Somehow my mouth said yes. My head and hands thought differently.

The day of the event arrived and my prayer was that the bra stayed up and the head/face piece didn't fall down. The lights came on and Siobhan Monique went on that stage and blew them away. And everything stayed in place. Success and Joy! And I found my new love. While I had always made big, bold, statement pieces with my jewelry, this metal clothing thing was a new realm and I was ready to jump in with both feet and both hands. And jump in, I did! Four months later, after seeing the metal bra, I was invited to be a runway artist at a well known wearable art fashion show and I created seven full metal clothing outfits. It went exceptionally well and new doors opened. I was making metal AND pushing women to accomplish their goals. I'd found the balance I was looking for. The integration was realized: SAYING and BEING and DOING. It was indeed possible.

At my first SPGB Coffee Talk, I wasn't nervous at all when I walked through those doors. I don't know why but I just wasn't. St Pete is truly magical for me, so I wasn't surprised. Now, I've been involved in my share of networking groups and women's groups and cultural groups. But this one was different from the start. The air felt different. The people felt different. The energy felt different. And let's be honest. I was different. I was 49. I knew ME better. I knew it was okay to be unapologetically multi-hyphenated. From the moment I walked in, I just felt like I belonged. It may have been because Havilah Vangroll made space for me to sit next to her at a table in the back of the room and we cut up like we'd known each other for 25 years. Or how from day one, my interactions with Sandy Bean, Kimberly Clark and Taylor Adams just felt genuine and supportive. This group of amazing women made a special effort to create a space that was intentionally inclusive. I can't begin to tell you what that means to me. As someone who has oftentimes NOT had that experience. SPGB always made me feel like it was okay to be me in every facet. To be me: multi-hyphenated. And, in fact, they helped me celebrate that. And because they gave me that space, I was able to do so, even before I felt like I was so.

The group isn't perfect. Heck, I wouldn't have felt like I belonged if it was. There are the cousins you're thrilled to see and those you hope simply wave from afar, and then there's the occasional crazy auntie we try to keep in the attic, but that's family, right? And that's what SPGB has been to me. Family. Plain and simple. Whether it's beach time with Lisa Alban or girl time after facials with Monique Fields or better understanding myself after a PQ Session with Kelly Abanda or unconditional support on so many levels from Megen Williams, I have chosen family in SPGB. Now I come from a dysfunctional family (like most of the world) so my view of family may be a little tilted, but I'm okay with that.

SPGB has shown up for me in a myriad of ways. From members who I never met showing up for a business promo photo shoot, to very last minute make up artist appointments before a tv interview, to Sandy Bean graciously extending her network to me and allowing me to represent SPGB on so many occasions. One of my favorite sayings is "show me your deeds and I'll tell you your ideology." I watch how the SPGB treats others. Mommas bringing babies find helpful hips to hold their children so they can go grab some tea and a breath. New comers are warmly greeted by the welcome wagon bearing sharpies and scones. Sacred spaces are held for those who may be struggling with something they hadn't even planned on divulging but felt safe enough to do so. Entrepreneurs have been born here. People are supported in their times of need. Opportunities to grow are encouraged. Silence is respected. And when come-to-Jesus discussions are needed, they are had. Collaboration over competition is real here. I know I may make this place sound mystical, like "where are the unicorns and fairy dust, Kamysha?" but if you look closely, I'm sure you'll find both on someone's socks or t-shirt.

I am Kamysha an Unapologetic-Pro Black-Woman-Metalsmith-Goal Coach-Metal Fashion Designer.

The definition of unapologetic is "in a manner that does not acknowledge or express regret" and that about sums it up for me.

Kamysha Martin *is an award-winning Metalsmith, Owner of lolahSoul Jewelry and Founder of SistahPush: Goal Coaching.*
www.SistahPush.com

Black women in business bring in just $24k in annual revenue on average. That is below the Federal poverty line for a household of four.

Question for Contemplation:
If you are a white woman, how can you change your business practices to be more inclusive of BIPOC women?

Pro Tip:
Most cities have a business bureau that lists businesses owned by marginalized communities, such as BIPOC-owned, women-owned, LGBTQ-owned.

Make patronizing these businesses your priority. And if your city doesn't have such a listing, create one!

FIVE
WATER IN THE DESERT

HAILEY RANK

"The sisterhood and support I received from my Girl Boss community was the best Girl Boss Effect I could have experienced."

BETWEEN THE GUT RATTLING HUNGER, THE HOSPITAL, and my husband almost dying a few days before New Year's Eve, I couldn't stay still. I was shivering, my hands making the faintest scratching sound as the pale desert that was my skin swishing as I fidgeted fearfully in the sterile environment of the ICU. I heard a beep that was different from the orchestra of tones coming out of blood pressure cuffs and heart monitors. It was a Facebook notification. Someone responded to my message in St. Pete Girl Boss. I was going to eat today.

I remember the first time I came to a *Friday Coffee* run by St. Pete Girl Boss. It wasn't something I just up and did. It took months of hearing about it through a couple friends, seeing posts at 9:45 am realizing I would definitely not make it in time, and then a couple of months of my son being in school for me to scrape myself from my excuses and go. I was late, coming from Largo, feeling a little frazzled and nervous. I was bringing my toddler, and I felt like I was heading to my first day of high school.

Were my clothes cute enough? Am I going to fit in? What if they don't like that I brought my baby. Am I enough of a business owner?

The last one was a pretty silly question, considering the fact that I *am* a business owner, and have been for a few years. As if the amount of revenue I made validated me as what I definitely am.

I thought I was going to learn about how to make my doula business better, and I have gained so much more. I have found myself, discovered new passions (and rediscovered old ones), and been supported through the hardest time of my entire life.

That first coffee meeting, we ended up going upstairs and were learning about ChatGPT. I was standing at a table, with my daughter in a buckle carrier on my back, swaying back and forth, passing cheddar bunnies over my shoulder to hands covered in cheesy crumbs. A bubbly woman (literally and figuratively- you'll see) at the table with us shared something about what she entered into ChatGPT, and in it she mentioned something about smile shirts.

I quietly asked, "Smile shirts? What do you do?"

She handed me a card, which read Carlyn Shaw, Smile Starter.

My mind practically exploded! I was inspired! I excitedly whispered, "I started The Smile Movement 12 years ago, passing out cards to make people smile and I called myself a smile maker!" I took this as a sign that I was in the right place. St. Pete Girl Boss was now a fixture in my life, little did I know how important it was.

She helped entertain my daughter with bubbles, because she's the type of person who hands out tiny tubes of bubbles to create joy. Little did she know, she re-ignited a flame inside of me. I hadn't made smile cards in years, and because of her I have made hundreds more. Smiles cards are printed on solar yellow paper, with reminders of how loved you are, and how worthy you are. I let people know that they are seen and appreciated. Solar yellow is bright, and fun, and yellow has been shown to make people happy.

The first time I handed them out, 12 years ago in downtown St. Pete, I saw a guy who I perceived as someone who would not be interested in my bubbly little cards. He had a grimace on his face, perpetually (or at least for the few minutes I was near him). I handed him one anyway. He chased me down through the park as I was handing them out.

"What's this on the back?" He said, pointing to a fraction of a line in the corner or the back of the card.

I showed him the other 3 cards with his, "When you come together, you create love," and the heart formed in the center of the cards. He got SO excited. He followed me around through the whole park, making sure everyone I handed them to knew what the mark on the back was for. That was a big lesson for me, and I am so grateful for it.

Giving people those moments of joy and love helped me realize that's what I want to do. Spreading joy has been at the heart of everything I've done over the years. Even the jobs I didn't love, I created joy for my coworkers and people on the phones. "Joy coach" was what I landed on as a profession about a week before my entire life got turned upside down, and I found out why Girl Boss would be truly life changing for me.

On December 28, 2023 my husband went to the ER because he was having chest pain, after what we thought was the cold or a flu. His fever wouldn't go down, and chest pain was the reason I said, "No, we need to go", because after googling it and reading in bold letters the number 1 reason to go in for a cold is CHEST PAIN, I didn't let him put it off. We got the kids fed, and drove to the ER. I had our daughter in the same buckle carrier, and our son sat in a chair playing his Nintendo Switch. My husband was not the type to exaggerate pain, and he also had a pretty high pain tolerance. They took him back for test after test, and back to the waiting room. He fell asleep in between tests. Then 8:30 came around and the kids were both falling asleep, too, so I took them home and got them washed and in bed, and practically threw the baby monitor to my grandfather.

I sped back to the hospital. They had him in an ER room, and hooked up to all of the monitors. His heart rate was so high, his oxygen was low (which was probably why he couldn't stay awake), and he was in TERRIBLE pain. He wanted to crawl out of his skin, to get up and walk around, but his oxygen just wouldn't come up, even on the highest flow. Getting out of that bed was the last thing he needed to be doing. One of the tests came back, along with the chest x-ray. He had pneumonia, and he was severely septic. They tried to see if the meds could work and he could calm down for the next couple hours.

The three-hour mark was approaching. Nothing was improving, and he was actually getting worse. At around midnight the ER doctor came in and told us that she thought my husband should have some medicine to rest... and be put on a ventilator to give his body a chance to heal.

As soon as he heard rest, after hours of being in pain, and the strongest pain medication not even touching it, he enthusiastically said yes. He also said yes to the ventilator, but it didn't get real until a minute or two later they brought all of those bags filled with accordion tubes and mouth pieces. They urgently had him sign several consent papers and then they started taking me to another room to wait. It all happened so fast that I almost got whisked away before saying bye to him. I turned and ran back, tears in my eyes because I needed to give him a kiss and I was praying with everything in my being that it wasn't a kiss goodbye.

I waited for the longest 3 hours of my life for them to get him to calm down with sedation, and in those three hours I unraveled. My best friend, and a few friends who I have made at St. Pete Girl Boss, began to show up for me on the digital realm. I went live and began sharing because it's all I could think to do. I also made a post in the Girl Boss group, asking for support in whatever way it could come. Sandy Bean immediately asked how she could support, and people lined up to help, asking about the kids and food and literally anything. An amazing Girl Boss named Nicole brought me food to the ICU, and sat with me and connected, until I felt like I really had to go back into the room because he might wake up or move or change... she made sure I didn't feel guilty for wanting to eat and run. She was graceful and loving in every sense of the words. She was the one who commented and brought me food on a day that I was just going to skip eating while I was there because I didn't want to leave his side.

The sisterhood and support I received from my Girl Boss

community was the best Girl Boss Effect I could have experienced. Women I hadn't even connected with aside from hellos or comments on posts, showed up at the hospital they transferred him to. I was given support in cleaning the house by an angel named Allyson Mixon who does so much more than cleaning houses, since I couldn't do anything in life aside from help my husband and tuck my kids in bed. Allyson came into my home and listened. She held safe space for me to process, and helped me clear physical space so my mental space could focus on the important things happening with my husband's health. She gave me a hug that felt like chicken noodle soup for my heart.

After 7 days, my husband was taken off the ventilator and just put on the only sedation you can be on without a ventilator until he could wake up calmly. By 11 days, he was being discharged from the hospital. And, an actual miracle, he is better than he was before he unknowingly must have had walking pneumonia.

Without the girl boss effect, I wouldn't have eaten most days, whether it was because someone brought me food, had it delivered, or simply reminded me to eat. I had friends checking in on me to make sure I was caring for *me* as I cared for everyone else, people lending ears, snacks, books, hugs, and childcare.

And, it hasn't been forgotten in the aftermath. When a life circumstance hits us like this, especially as business owners, it can be astronomically difficult to pick back up where your business was. I have tried beating myself up, and getting caught in comparison, and even had an emotional breakdown at our Galentine's event. When I started crying when someone asked how I was, because trauma is weird, I was met with love. One friend, Kelly Abanda, helped me breathe into my feelings, and feel safe in my body. Reminding me that it's okay to not be okay. She helped me breathe, as I processed the days my husband couldn't.

The founder, Sandy Bean, a chaotic ball of grace and power, found me and brought me to a more private part of the venue, in the actual theater, and sat with me as I processed everything. It wasn't until reflecting that I realized how special that made me feel. It was her organization's event. She stole away to come help me through a moment of PTSD. Not once did it feel like high school. I was cared for and loved the way that I had needed my whole life. There was no judgment, only empathy and encouragement, and meeting me where I was at.

For me, the Girl Boss Effect has been so much deeper than my business, it has been a journey of the soul. It has been finding my purpose in life, and my place in a community. When I entered the desert of my life, St. Pete Girl Boss brought me water. Literally and figuratively.

Hailey Rank *is a creative mom of two on a mission to bring the world more joy and smiles, inspired by the childlike wonder and love for those around the world. She does that through writing on her blog and in her books and guided journals, through her YouTube, and by handing out little pieces of paper she calls "smile cards."*

Women entrepreneurs pay themselves 28% less than white cisgender men.

Question for Contemplation:
How do you determine what to charge, and what to pay yourself?

Pro Tip:
Consider increasing what you charge for your services and products.

Experiment with increasing your fees by 50% simply by writing it and naming it aloud the next time someone asks you the cost.

SIX
AN UNEXPECTED TRANSFORMATION

LISA ALBAN

"My business mindset has transformed from one of exploration to one of strategic growth and innovation."

It was a beautiful Friday morning, and the room was filled with the vibrant energy of female entrepreneurs. As I walked into the local coffee shop, I felt a mix of excitement and anticipation. The founders of St. Pete Girl Bosses (SPGB) had agreed to join me for an episode of the Conscious Collaboration Podcast. My co-host Emily and I often turned to the ancient wisdom of the I Ching to guide our discussions and share meaningful insights with our listeners. On this day, the message of Revolution and community emerged. The synchronicity was remarkable; it felt as if the ancient oracle was speaking directly to the heart of SPGB. The Zoom room was filled with a palpable sense of magic as we delved into the transformative power of community and collaboration. This wasn't just another podcast episode; it embodied the very essence of SPGB. We laughed, shared stories, and envisioned a future where our combined efforts would lead to profound change.

From that day, my involvement with SPGB deepened. I found myself surrounded by like-minded women who not only understood my journey but were also eager to support and uplift each other. We played together, worked together, and grew together. The connections I made were not just professional; they became some of my closest friendships. This sense of belonging and mutual support was nothing short of revolutionary for me and my business.

The WHY Behind My Business

My journey into the world of Feng Shui and Quantum Energy Alignment deepened during a transformative period in my life. Having experienced a career shift, the joy of welcoming a new baby, and then facing the challenges of Covid and divorce, I found myself genuinely reconnecting with my true self. It was during this time that I launched Cloud 9 Feng Shui LLC and co-founded the Intrinsic School of Feng Shui. This phase was not one of sadness but of rebirth and growth. My energy was boundless, and I was seeking like-minded individuals who were growth-oriented, collaborative, playful, and fearless.

I started my business with a personal mission to guide others toward healing and transformation through the power of Feng Shui and energetics. My business story is one of resilience and empowerment. Over the years, I have honed my skills and expanded my offerings to include comprehensive interior design services that create harmonious and supportive environments for my clients. My personal WHY is deeply rooted in my desire to make a difference in people's lives, helping them find balance and strength during their most expansive times.

My design philosophy is deeply rooted in Modern Feng Shui energetic assessment. Each consultation begins with understanding the unique story of each client and their environment. This approach allows me to create spaces that not only reflect their beautiful energy but also support their deepest goals and dreams. Unlike a one-size-fits-all approach, I do not create the "LISA ALBAN look." Instead, I tailor my designs to emulate the essence of my clients, fostering an environment where they can truly thrive.

Business BEFORE SPGB

Before I became involved with SPGB, my business was at a crossroads. I had established a solid foundation but felt a deep yearning for a community of like-minded, growth-oriented women. The entrepreneurial journey, especially as a female business owner, often felt isolated. I yearned for a community where I could share my experiences, seek advice, and find the support that I desperately needed.

My initial encounter with SPGB was through a local networking event. The warmth and openness of the members were immediately apparent. I was drawn to the group's ethos of collaboration and support. My first few interactions were filled with meaningful conversations and genuine connections. It was clear that this was a space where I could thrive both personally and professionally. Prior to joining SPGB, my business mindset was one of exploration. I was focused on expanding my client base and exploring new opportunities but lacked a broader vision for strategic growth. There was a constant undercurrent of excitement and potential. However, the encouragement and resources I found within SPGB started to shift my perspective.

Life and Business AFTER SPGB

Today, the status of my work is more robust and dynamic than ever before. My business mindset has transformed from one of exploration to one of strategic growth and innovation. The support and mentorship I've received from SPGB have empowered me to take bold steps, expand my services, and reach new heights. I now approach my business with a sense of confidence and clarity that was previously missing.

One pivotal resource that SPGB brought to my attention was the Jim Moran Institute for Global Entrepreneurship through Florida State University. If it weren't for SPGB, I wouldn't have been made aware of the program, and I wouldn't have applied. I was accepted into the Spring Cohort of Small Business Executives and received 8 weeks of upleveled information and connections that helped me to scale my business with current training resources, expert guidance, and networking. The program provided me with invaluable insights into business strategies and operations, which have been instrumental in the growth and sustainability of Cloud 9 Feng Shui.

The tangible results are evident in the increased revenue and client base of Cloud 9 Feng Shui. But beyond the numbers, the most profound change has been in my personal sense of fulfillment and connection. I feel a deep sense of belonging within the SPGB community. The collaborations and friendships I've formed have enriched my life in ways I never imagined. The magic of SPGB lies in its ability to bring together women who inspire and uplift each other, creating an environment where we can all thrive.

One of the most exciting collaborations was with fellow Girl Boss Nicole Simpson. Together, we crafted an amazing workshop combining Feng Shui and Human Design. Our motto was "Why be a shooting star when you can be a Galaxy?" Our intention was to help others connect with their best Human Design partners for collaboration in their business and to integrate Feng Shui principles uniquely prescribed to each collaborative team. Nicole and I enjoy joining forces to share our wisdom, knowledge, and experience to uplevel entrepreneurs and collaborative teams with our methods. When entrepreneurs align our services with what lights us up, we really shine in a way that radiates. I look forward to future events showcasing our method!

Words of Wisdom

To my fellow girl bosses, I offer this advice: Embrace the power of community and collaboration. Surround yourself with those who believe in you and your vision. The journey of entrepreneurship is filled with challenges, but with the support of a community like SPGB, you can overcome any obstacle and achieve extraordinary success. This community spirit aligns with my work with High Vibe Entrepreneurial Women and the Conscious Collaboration Podcast and Collective, as well as my role as the Board Chair of the International Feng Shui Guild.

These communities are great examples of the Period 9 revolution in full effect. Period 9 is a significant era in Feng Shui, representing a time of revolution and a shining moment for women, especially those in their middle age. It emphasizes the rise of feminine attributes, emotional intelligence, collaboration, community, and the nurturing of self and others. The SPGB group has exemplified these qualities, helping to introduce me to wonderful women, forging friendships, and integrating me more with the entrepreneurial vibe of St. Petersburg, Florida.

We are in an age of Revolution, and I hope everyone is ready for it. Remember, we are stronger together. Why be a shooting star when you can be a Galaxy?

Lisa Alban, *Feng Shui Master Designer, Trainer, and Energy Alignment Practitioner, transforms spaces and lives. www.cloud9fengshui.com.*

Only 24% of "experts" cited in the media are women.

Question for Contemplation:
What are your areas of expertise and how can you better share your wisdom with the world?

Pro Tip:
Don't limit your understanding of "expert" to someone who has a Ph.D. in the field. Consider your expertise, experience, and enthusiasm and how each of these elements of your life make you an expert in many areas.

SEVEN
A HEALER'S PERSPECTIVE

MELANIA MERSADES

"My greatest challenge as a multi-dimensional healer has been allowing myself to be seen...The Girl Boss Frequency made it hard to remain unnoticed."

BEING A LEARNED EXPERIENCE EXPERT ON ENERGY Medicine and the paranormal has been a lonely path.

My greatest challenge as a multi-dimensional healer has been allowing myself to be seen and revered. I'm working through false humility. A journey that ultimately led me to discover the transformative power of true community and collaboration, particularly through my involvement with the Saint Pete Girl Bosses.

Having a calling placed over my life in my childhood years wasn't easy. Being born gifted often left me feeling isolated, driven by questions about why people get sick and why healing doesn't always happen.

Exploring the unseen realms and unknown takes up

most of my time. I'm not afraid to speak truth or share my feelings. Shying away from conflict or discomfort isn't part of my personality. These traits make me effective in my profession. For me to engage, it has to be worth my time.

In this capitalistic society, where I've monetized my innate abilities, I realized that scaling my business requires a community that understands and values me, allowing me to fully express myself creatively.

In 2020, my business was at the height of its success even after the announcement of the Covid Crisis. I taught more classes on Energy Mastery, sold more Essential Oils and initiated more students into Reiki than all previous years combined. But I still lacked an entrepreneurial community.

Have you ever felt pressured to fit into a mold that doesn't align with who you are? For me, it wasn't just about scaling my business—it was about staying true to myself while making an even larger impact.

I prayed for a networking group aligned with my values.

In 2021, as the world became increasingly addicted to illicit drugs and abusing sacred plant medicines like ayahuasca, guidance was sought from spirit to find a way that would support clients in purging their emotions more swiftly. The path led to the study of dessert medicine [Sananga] and the traditional medicine of the people, tobacco snuff [Hapé]. I am Puerto Rican.

Traveling to Peru for an initiation marked the beginning of a profound healing journey that connected me with my roots.

Sananga sharpens perception; clearing physical & energetic blockages, while Hapé grounds the mind, aligns chakras, and promotes emotional clarity. The synergy between these two helped me quantum leap beyond what my body had been holding onto.

Integration and embodiment of the teachings required significant time and reflection, ultimately leading me to apply these insights in both individual and group healing sessions, as well as in ceremonial settings.

By October 2021, a paradigm shift occurred within me that made me feel ready to connect on a larger scale. I joined a women's business group that nurtured true sisterhood and met my unique needs as a Latina. Coming out of my shell felt freeing yet the need to expand beyond my comfort levels was a priority.

When the SPGB group emerged in 2022, I was skeptical due to past betrayals and failed collaborations. I've had to deal with intellectual property theft and sisterhoods that became nothing more than mean girls of St Pete.

Initially, the label "GIRL BOSS" didn't sit right with me. I felt it was limiting & didn't reflect my identity as an Indigo Warrior. It might be because I belong to Generation X that I dislike labels. Getting me to subscribe to one takes a lot of work! Have you ever locked yourself into a label or accolades that limited your growth?

Online interactions felt superficial reinforcing my hesitancy. The energy just seemed off. I declined invitations to attend in person with a 'no thank you, I don't need to be in a circle of fake females welcoming me in just to steal my ideas then cancel me again' mindset. I also didn't want to be the token Latina.

That struggle is real.

If you knew the emotional challenges I've faced with false tribes, spiritual bypassers, and abusive "leaders," you'd understand my reluctance. Sandy Bean and the Girl Boss team encouraged me to attend in person, promising a different experience.

For 2 years, I observed from the sidelines, intrigued by Sandy's leadership and her alignment with my values. I caught a live video once where she put a name to what I had been experiencing; R.S.D. Rejection Sensitive Dysphoria. It kept me locked into P.assing O.ver O.pportunity R.epeatedly. How? Because being excluded intentionally was a trigger for me. Raging as to the reasons why women couldn't just work together used to be my norm.

Sandy's knowledge regarding people with attention deficit hyperactivity was providing me some relief, inspiring me to make changes. I feel better in the company of someone who gets me!

A friend who took my suggestion and attended one of Sandy's trainings gave me inspirational feedback. It helped me approach the decision with less resistance.

Who am I, really? My name is Melania Mersades and I am a soulful, playful, visionary leader. I'm known as a spiritual badass and grateful to be alive! My leadership style is intuitive. My main focus is to connect, create, and collaborate. I know that I'm an asset to any team or project, but the world doesn't yet know!

I've worked one-on-one with over 30,000 people and logged more than 13,000 hours in energy-focused bodywork. There are now massage schools that teach what I've learned through hands-on experience. That's my current dream, to create a massage school.

There's a need for education on spiritual exploration, self-healing, and massage, which I prioritize teaching. Yet there's still a lot of need for self care, self love, and pain relief.

Not just physical pain, spiritual pain, which is why I provide healing services.

Could I be a Girl Boss?

Full transparency: when in my shadow, my inner thoughts run rampant left unchecked. When thinking about attending in person, my mind would replay old stories. "Surely they will reject me!" Before deciding to attend I became a leader for the other networking group and falsely believed I would be rejected for this reason, as well. Of course, I was wrong but I didn't know that at the time of deciding.

As a Shadow Worker, I understand that overly protecting my heart can hinder my growth. Despite this, Spirit guided me to embrace opportunities, recognizing that my presence & skills could benefit others.

In my role as a lightworker, I teach the Art of Spiritual Badasserie℠, a comprehensive approach that blends energy healing, awareness, and mastery through modalities like Reiki, Aroma, Color, Sound, Music, and Massage. This process, honed over decades, includes vibrational healing with crystal and Nepalese bowls, which brings about mutually beneficial peace.

With over 31 years in alternative medicine and self-improvement, I've gathered deep insights into healing and self-love. I now share this knowledge through Reiki Certification, Spa Days, couples massage classes and workshops both on-line and in person. This multifaceted approach not only reflects my journey but also addresses the diverse needs of those I work with, ensuring a holistic and memorable experience.

In January of 2024, the energy of SPGB had also shifted. With a beginner's mind, open heart, and willing spirit, I approached my first Girl Boss meeting determined to try something new.

If you've never been to Friday Coffee, you may get addicted within the first 15 minutes.

That was me!

The energy at the welcome table is always genuinely inviting. I know this because I can spot fake energy easily. I briskly waved and smiled, then introduced myself to the first woman I encountered.

Typically, I enter feminine spaces cautiously. From the moment I stepped into NOVA, I knew I had to shift behaviors to generate the results I was hoping for.

The Girl Boss Frequency made it hard to remain unnoticed.

The topic of discussion was "How to prompt ChatGPT." I wanted to advance my skills in using artificial intelligence. I hold strict boundaries with this technology. Sandy showed me how to make it work for me.

I got a taste of the Girl Boss Effect and wanted more. It took me a few weeks to process my initial meeting. Being an energy intuitive I integrate with what I've learned before taking in more.

Oh, I definitely went back.

During one of the meetings, Sandy shared a term with more than 50 women in attendance that perfectly describes my reluctance: toxic feminism. To personally experience how Girl Boss aims to challenge these destructive forces, I had to keep showing up.

The solutions put forth in her talk align with my global mission. Together, I believe we can collectively feel our way into a better world.

By February 2024, one simple post in the online group

A HEALER'S PERSPECTIVE

led to a solid connection and collaboration. Thanks to SPGB, I quickly found a studio space with another Girl Boss, which allowed me to acquire what I had been searching for: my own private studio space.

Finally, the Girl Boss Effect lit me up!

I'm eager to share my healing gifts with this community, especially with those who value wellness and align with my vision of building a nurturing community. Although I'm still breaking out of my shell, SPGB feels like my "work home", where I can contribute to a supportive, collaborative, and prosperous legacy.

Meeting Sandy in person and participating in SPGB events shifted my perspective on collaborations. Every meeting I attend, I become more intrigued and satisfied. By just being itself, this community is helping me forgive the past and heal so that I can continue leveling up.

One of the main benefits is feeling seen, loved, and valued.

I joined the annual membership in June and am benefiting from the VIP bonuses. The Thursday zoom meetings and Tuesday co-work hours provide clarity and confirmation. I have experienced so much transformation in such a short amount of time that allowing myself to be seen and revered is becoming a lot easier.

I was invited to teach during the July 26, extended coffee and my subject was, The Human Energy Field Demystified. I got excellent feedback. I also accomplished some professional goals with this membership perk and made some more connections.

On August 30th, I woke up feeling refreshed and renewed, like a weight had lifted. Yet there was still something stirring within me that made me hesitate in deciding to attend this day's Friday Coffee. I dragged myself to that meeting.

During the opening, Sandy mentioned the other business networking group, and my Co-Leader Elāna Rheinhart shouted out the details. Then the newest meeting leaders quickly shouted out their details. And I immediately got super emotional, excused myself from the table and rushed to the bathroom for an emotional release.

As I cried, I looked at myself in the mirror, noticed red eyes and immediately thought to myself, "You made up a story about how you would be rejected based on your past experiences and robbed yourself of potential opportunities. Let this be the last time!"

It was a moment of personal evolution for me. The clarity was in my mind while the tears came rolling down my face. The evidence finally arrived to prove how wrong I had been. If I hadn't shown up this day, I would have only heard about it. I would have missed this healing opportunity.

We are doing it. We are truly working together for a better today and an even better tomorrow.

If you are struggling with inner pain or mean girl energy, I highly recommend one of the solutions I've offered in this essay.

If you have a valid reason for not attending a women's business networking group, I feel you. I suggest that you investigate further and measure whether their mission aligns with your goals as a business owner. Are you a solo-prenuer tired of being solo? Like me, you'll have to work through that inner resistance. If you happen to live near the SPGB meeting in Saint Pete Florida, I highly encourage you to attend.

If you have been to the Friday Coffee and wondering

who I am, I'm the one singing & dancing during the wins section. Come dance and celebrate with me!

I'm proudly embracing the label of Girl Boss. I'm not just any Girl Boss; I'm a Latina Girl Boss! To be continued...

Melania Mersades is an award-winning Licensed Massage Therapist, Author, and Ceremonialist. As the founder of Melania's Healing Edge, she integrates ancient wisdom with modern techniques to promote holistic living and spiritual growth. She is also the creator of Beach Reiki Tampa Bay, now celebrating eight years of dedicated community service.
www.melaniashealingedge.com

78% of self-employed women hit an income wall of $50k
per year and never rise above that amount.

Question for Contemplation:
How much money do you need to earn to live your dream life?

Pro Tip:
Get out your journal or open a spreadsheet depending on
your preference. Take ten minutes to write down every
element of your dream life.

Want a fairy cottage in the middle of the woods, a high rise condo overlooking the beach, or a 4-bedroom with a playroom and home office so there's plenty of room for the whole family?

Want to travel, have a private chef, donate to all your favorite causes?

Write it down.

Now, do some research. Find out how much it costs to have each element of your dream life.

This is the first step toward creating the life of your dreams.

EIGHT
EMBRACING COLLABORATION: HOW THE GIRL BOSS EFFECT TRANSFORMED MY LIFE

LISA ANN MARONE

"Despite my professional feats, imposter syndrome was my not-so-silent partner."

MY LIFE HAS BEEN A WHIRLWIND OF HATS – DEDICATED mom, loving wife, educator extraordinaire, and HR guru. It all kicked off with a degree in Behavior Disorders, leading me into the trenches of Special Education. For four years, I lived in a world where patience wasn't just a virtue, it was a survival skill. But in 2002, when I was expecting my son, the stress of the job made my husband and me rethink our choices.

So, I pivoted. Supporting my husband's law practice became my new gig, sliding into the HR role (turns out, wrangling lawyers isn't much different from managing a classroom of kids with behavioral disorders – who knew?). For over a decade, I juggled business ops while moonlighting as a volunteer for local nonprofits. But when the law firm shuttered in 2020, I was at a crossroads, itching to carve out something uniquely mine. Enter PEACE in the Burg – my brainchild to bolster small businesses and nonprofits in St. Petersburg through cause marketing, publishing, and event wizardry.

Despite my professional feats, imposter syndrome was my not-so-silent partner. Growing up, watching my mom's friends compete rather than collaborate left me wary of other women. This skepticism stuck, making it tough to ask for or accept help. That all changed with St. Pete Girl Boss.

Heather Hamar kept inviting me to Friday coffee meetups. She sold it as "a dynamic sisterhood of collaboration over competition," but I was skeptical. Plus, the thought of driving downtown on a Friday morning without guaranteed parking – no thanks. But the universe had other plans. When the group outgrew their downtown digs, Heather suggested using the St. Petersburg City Theatre, where I was already volunteering. It was kismet. I skulked around the office pretending to work until I finally attended a meeting. The warmth and genuine support I encountered were game-changing. These women celebrated each other's wins and gave feedback with kindness.

One of my first encounters was with Kelly Abanda, who was borrowing chairs from the theatre. We clicked instantly, and when I opened up about my background, her empathy and insight were like a balm. Another transformative moment came during a Human Design workshop led by Shakti Rios. Her confidence and encouragement to "own our story" helped me unearth parts of myself I'd long ignored.

The Girl Boss Effect extended beyond individual mentorship. It created a sense of belonging I hadn't felt before. Networking events became rich with insights and camaraderie, building a support network that always had my back. A standout collaboration has been with Erica Holland of The Roaming Petal and Heather Hamar from The Mar. Together, we birthed Blooms Day, an event that fills the streets with flowers and joy. It started with a simple question about May Day and blossomed into an annual celebration.

The most significant change, though, was internal. My imposter syndrome began to fade. Watching these women face their fears and forge ahead was inspiring. Their resilience taught me to embrace my imperfections.

Thanks to continuous engagement with St. Pete Girl Boss, I learned to celebrate even my smallest wins. Compliments and critiques became easier to accept, knowing they came from a place of genuine support.

The Girl Boss Effect has opened doors I never knew existed, showing me that collaboration trumps competition any day. Through St. Pete Girl Boss, I've found my voice, my community, and, most importantly, my peace.

Lisa Marone *has spent over 15 years connecting, volunteering, event planning, promoting and friend/fundraising for her favorite non-profits in St Petersburg and St Pete Beach. Her PR and communications organization PEACE In The Burg connects local businesses with nonprofits for collaborative cause related marketing, and she serves as the Front of the House VP for the St Pete City Theatre. www.peaceintheburg.com*

29% of American firms are owned by women, yet employ only 6% of the country's workforce and account for barely 4% of business revenues.

Question for Contemplation:
What is preventing you from hiring an additional person to work with you?

Pro Tip:
Consider bartering services to get what you need as your business grows. Make sure to get agreements in writing and barter equal value goods and services so expectations are very clear and everyone gets the support they desire in a way that can work very well for everyone.

NINE
MY PERSONAL GIRL BOSS EFFECT

KATHY HOUSTON

"We are not alone. We are not a hot mess. We are strong. We are valuable. We will succeed and we are enough. Building these relationships in an open and vulnerable environment is the secret in the sauce. The secret sauce that is the Girl Boss Effect."

HAVE YOU EVER HEARD OF THAI MASSAGE? *WHAT IS that*, I wondered. After meeting Brenda at the Friday Coffee, I couldn't wait to find out. A tall unassuming woman with a big smile and an even bigger hug, Brenda was a genuinely joyful person. Her happy personality radiated peace and calm. "What is this Thai Massage and where do I sign up?" I blurted out. Brenda and I exchanged our business information and cards. Another Girl Boss commented at our round table discussion that Brenda was very goofy and she highly recommended her. That's it... I was hooked. I signed up on Brenda's schedule right after the meeting.

I found her cute little studio on Central Ave. A very calming and serene environment greeted all my senses. Brenda took time to ask and hear my needs. As a regular client of chiropractic and many massages, I was very curious about this "Thai" technique. It did not disappoint. Brenda was very skillful with stretching, kneading, and massage all on a cushion on the floor. Breathe in breath out—all out—Ahhhh! Very effective release of tension, tightness, and negative energy. I could tell Brenda loved her craft. It was a blessing that she got to give to others. What a great business model: Do something you love for the benefit of others and get paid.

That's why I started my Run Your Life Coaching business just a few short years ago. My own personal story compelled me to leave retail and strike out on my own. At the age of 50 I went through a messy and difficult time that took several years to reconcile the self-doubt, the guilt, the anger, and even shame. I was not happy in my long-time marriage to my husband and I didn't know why. Something was missing, I was not whole, fulfilled or joyful. Then while training in Chicago I met HER. Bazinga! Whoop there it is! And now what do I do? I had to be true to myself and accept the consequences of who I deeply am a LILLE—Late In Life Lesbian. Ugly arguments, accusations, jealousy, and resentment poured out as my husband and I tried to figure what to do. I left after 35 years of marriage and joined my now wife.

This is what propelled me into a coaching career to help other women be true to themselves; understanding their why, their purpose and ultimately themselves. As we hit those mid-life years, so many transitions are bombarding us: menopause, empty-nest, divorce, career changes, financial

MY PERSONAL GIRL BOSS EFFECT

concerns, and grandchildren to name a few. The mental and physical fatigue takes a toll on our relationships and careers. We question our entire being and our purpose as we enter this second chapter of life.

I completed the Coach Training Alliance certification course online with live practice coaching calls and some business acumen. I had no idea what it took to run a business and hopped from free courses to free live seminars trying to find the answer. I spent a bunch of money on what I thought would help with some results. I did all the basics and then struggled with lead generation, where are my people and how do I get warm leads and potential clients. I floundered around with online groups and courses, still not getting it. As I moved into a full time focus on business development, I searched business networking events on EventBrite. Many organizations came up and I started signing up and traveling back to Tampa and networking my ass off. It was exhausting and expensive. I still wasn't with my people. So, I changed my search to Women's business networking events. Now, I was onto something. Ahh hah! Moment. Which one? I tried several of the groups and gave them a shot. Free was definitely for me. So, St Pete Girl Bosses met for a free Friday coffee very close to my house.

I went into Nova 535, not knowing what to expect. I knew no one. Let's just check this one out, I thought to myself. I was instantly greeted and welcomed. "Oh, you are new, here is a name tag and here is some coffee and we are so glad you are here." Okayyyy! You've got my attention now. Several women came up and introduced themselves and we exchanged cards and chatted about our businesses. There were other members of the LGBTQ+ community. That's an important piece for me. Then we were called to our seats by this crazy, funny, and amazing person. Later I would learn that this persona was the founder and creator, Sandy Bean. She introduced "Barbara Barker" and everyone was yelling and cheering and saying "BFD". I'm listening and I'm thinking are we really yelling the F word. Hell Yes, I have found my people. What a great vibe and high energy, I'm in.

So, the Girl Boss Effect, as we call it, is when we help each other in any way. Collaborations, referrals, and ideas are all shared freely and openly. The Friday coffees are not just about networking. They are so much more. I have learned valuable information for my business about Google, SEO, and software. I have met exciting women in similar spaces and we have worked on our Facebook together and learned about Facebook Ads. We had financials round robins about insurance, taxes, and business credit. I met with Angela, aka Barbara Barker, about how to build business credit.

The real secret in the sauce is the energy, community and safe space that has been created for like minded women building their businesses. Sandy Bean has created and built this community and built a team to carry it forward. To her credit when Sandy was out due to a medical situation the "show" went on without her. Her zany ADHD antics were missed and we continued on with her vision and her passion.

We are not alone. We are not a hot mess. We are strong. We are valuable. We will succeed and we are enough. Building these relationships in an open and vulnerable environment is the secret in the sauce. The secret sauce that is the Girl Boss Effect.

Kathy Houston *is a US Army Veteran and Positive Intelligence Coach known as the Run Your Life Coach. She specializes in helping women who want to make a difference by sharing their gifts and talents with the world.*
www.runyourlife.biz

Women are 80% more likely to be impoverished in retirement than men.

Question for Contemplation:
How does scarcity mindset impact your earning potential? How does it impact enjoying your money?

Pro Tip:
Money Mindset is a constant process. Spend time cultivating feelings of safety and gratitude around money, including checking balances regularly, being intentional about noticing money coming in and being grateful for the ability to give or cover your expenses. The more positive experiences you can create around earning, the more space you will have available for financial success.

TEN
IGNITING MY SPARK

NYLA WILLIAMS

"I am part of a statistic that made me feel I was destined for failure...My dream was to show that my past does not define me. Instead, it serves as a catalyst to demonstrate to others YOU create your own destiny."

IT WAS ALREADY 8:41 AM. ANOTHER FRIDAY MORNING I let slip out of my fingertips... I could not be the one to show up late. A sense of anxiety flowed through my entire body, I could feel myself getting worked up. The meeting would be filled with highly successful, immensely knowledgeable, and unusually intimidating female entrepreneurs. I was a nobody. Nobodies don't attend their first meeting and make a solid lasting impression by being late. These doubts and insecurities crowded my mind, I almost let anxiety consume me. Walking towards the entrance. Stopping. Turning around. Back to my car. Walking towards the entrance. Stopping.

Turning around. Back to my car. Stuck in what felt like a never ending cycle. I must have looked foolish. I paused for a brief moment to think, "What if I go in there and it changes everything?"

So I did.

And it did.

I opened the door to see at least 75 beautiful women from all different walks of life gathered together. "Maybe I'm in the wrong place?" I thought to myself. I should have felt overwhelmed by this encounter but instead a smile slowly grew across my face and I felt light as air as the energy in the room was indescribably blissful. To an outsider the energy may have seemed tumultuous yet on a deeper level it was simply serene with authentic interactions happening all around. I could feel the positive energy flowing throughout the room as these women connected and engaged with one another. It felt like a breath of fresh air, no judgmental eyes looking in my direction. I could just be me. I walked up to a table on the side of the room, unsure of what to do next. The sweetest woman with a bubbly disposition greeted me, Taylor Adams. A first conversation that would throw out all doubts and insecurities I once had. I introduced myself to her, mentioning this was my first GB coffee softly saying, "Hi. I'm Nyla, a professional organizer and owner of NylaVen Designs." Without hesitation she gave the biggest smile exclaiming, "We're so glad you are here, thank you for joining us!" "That was it?" I thought to myself. I was already "in," I did not need to prove my worth or my value to be welcomed here. I felt astounded.

This was not just an ordinary networking event; it was a transformative moment. Within minutes, introductions led to opportunities. I felt an overwhelming sense of belonging

IGNITING MY SPARK

and hope. It was a domino effect and within 15 minutes I had more potential clients and possible new friends than I had made in the last year of my business. By the end of the meeting I had rediscovered my passion and commitment to my business, NylaVen Designs. I felt hopeful for the first time. Hopeful, that I would not be forced to get a 9 to 5 after graduation. Hopeful, that I would not be alone as a female entrepreneur. Hopeful, that I would have the chance to change people's lives with my organization business. That was it. I went into that meeting and it changed everything, it changed me. I had gotten my SPARK back and I haven't looked back since.

A spark that initially ignited from a young age, where I had all the odds stacked against me. I mean, I was just a girl navigating the world with an ACE score of 10. A daunting number describing adverse childhood experiences that could impact a child's future. ACE scores explore the impacts of traumatic childhood adversities ranging from abuse and neglect to family dysfunction. According to Montana State University, an ACE score of 4 or more makes an individual 1220% more likely to attempt suicide and 460% more likely to develop depression. I am part of a statistic that made me feel I was destined for failure. The world is not set up for people like me. Not a piece of my story I share often, but it's the driving force behind my motivation. In my childhood, I faced more adversity and trauma than any person should ever have to experience in their lifetime. People told me I would not amount to anything coming from a broken home. The world tries to make you believe that your past, your circumstances, and your background will decide your future, but they don't – you do.

My dream is to show that my past does not define me.

Instead, it serves as a catalyst to demonstrate to others YOU create your own destiny. Growing up in a tumultuous environment, I always felt overwhelmed and out of control. It inspired me to find a way to create order and stability. By learning how to transform my own chaotic surroundings, I discovered I could help others who felt as lost and burdened as I once did. I've always loved helping those around me and have an eye for seeing the potential regardless of the barriers. My personal history, of overcoming adversity, deeply influences how I approach organization. I understand the emotional toll living in chaos can take and know some people need that empathetic guide to help them reach their goal. That's what led me to start NylaVen Designs, a professional organization business, dedicated to helping others find their safe space through organization. I take a compassionate and efficient approach that is tailored to each client's needs as the organization project is completed. I knew through my business I could share my gift and my goal was simple: To turn the struggle and disorder I faced into a service that could transform lives by providing a sense of control and calm.

One of my most transformative moments with my business was collaborating with a beautiful soul, Alyssa VanNuys, a fellow organizer. We met through SPGB and I immediately knew we needed to connect. She served as a mentor for me, being well established with her business she offered insightful and career changing advice that allowed me to grow my business. Throughout the past two years, I have gained a lifelong business companion and friend, who only wants to see me succeed. We decided to collaborate on a pro-bono organization project for a foster family who felt weighed down with the disorder in their home. They struggled with feeling drained from constant tidying and felt stuck on how to implement lasting solutions. I felt called to be part of this project as I witnessed first hand the daily chaos and stress overwhelmed parents faced, during my career as a nanny. We were able to get three girl bosses together, each with their own organization business, to incorporate our individual techniques to help change the lives of this family. These interactions are what set SPGB apart, it's about collaboration not competition. It's about transforming lives and sharing what each individual girl boss has to offer the world, not just about being "successful."

My past experiences ignited my passion for helping others find order in their homes and freeing them from the mental burden disorganization brings. Disorganization is something that impacts your day-to-day life and becomes an impossible task to even consider starting. When your home is a mess it affects your stress, it consumes your time, and it leaves you feeling stuck. I give people back their safe space by taking this huge weight off of them and freeing them from the burden of a messy home. It's my personal mission to give people a home they can thrive in, allowing them to have more time to put into things they enjoy. At NylaVen Designs I work with clients to design and implement organization systems that fit their individual needs. My goal is not just to declutter your physical space but also your mind. By establishing effective and easy-to-maintain systems, you are able to reclaim your time and energy, enabling you to focus on what truly matters to you. I love taking this unique approach to ensure my clients homes remain a sanctuary of peace and productivity, adapting as their needs evolve over time.

Despite the passion I had for NylaVen Designs, I once struggled to see its potential impact and often questioned its value. Even after graduating with a bachelor's in business management, I thought NylaVen Designs would amount to nothing. I used to call my "little business" a side hustle and brush it off as nothing important. SPGB has inspired me to pursue my passion of entrepreneurship. The warmth and encouragement from this community helped me see the true worth of my business. I was no longer just helping people declutter their homes; I was offering them a chance to reclaim their mental space and find joy in their lives. The "Girl Boss Magic" provided me with invaluable connections and insights that helped propel NylaVen Designs forward, allowing me to grow and make a meaningful difference in my clients' lives. I used to let the world make me believe my accomplishments were sheer luck and not practical in the long run.

How was I so wrong? NylaVen Designs is going places and is a business worth investing time into. I believe in myself and know that my success is not because I got lucky, it's because I'm a big fucking deal and there is no one like me. Every single time I leave a meeting I feel inspired and privileged to be in the presence of brilliant and powerful women, who are not afraid of being vulnerable. This community transformed what it means to me to be an entrepreneur and helped me learn there is so much more to it than money and success. SPGB's support was instrumental in my ability to expand my client base, refine my services, and reinforce my belief in my own worth and the value I offer.

Before SPGB I had not had a single client that was not family or a close friend. I downplayed my worth and value, believing that "anyone can be an organizer so why would anyone pay me to do it for them." I would do projects for free or ask for a minimal fee which led me to work with people who did not appreciate my gift. At one point, I gave up on my business applying for the 9 to 5 jobs which I dreaded with all of my soul. Honestly, this ultimately led me to my first Girl Boss meeting. The meeting was the deciding factor on whether or not I would give up my dream of becoming an entrepreneur. The meeting where a fire started in me, where I got my spark back and remembered why I started my business in the first place. Through the past two years the knowledge and wisdom I've gained has taught me how to advocate for my worth and not allow others to take it from me.

Through consistently attending meetings and gaining connections, I now get multiple client leads on a weekly basis. Whether that's through a referral from a Girl Boss in the Facebook group, Friday morning coffees or even through connections made with friends of Girl Bosses, I gain new connections almost daily and get to expand my circle. I am able to charge my worth as I know the value of my talent. In fact, I had my highest month of revenue since beginning my business in July of 2024 bringing in over $4,000 in profits. I worked with four new clients and had two returning clients who trusted me to organize their safe spaces. I can hire additional help for bigger projects, which is something I never thought I would be able to do. I gain at least one new client a month and even have returning clients that reach out, because they loved the work I did so much. It almost feels like I am living in a dream, my dream of not allowing my past to define who I could become but allowing it to be my greatest opportunity to show others I have created my own destiny.

NYLA WILLIAMS

Nyla Williams *is the owner of NylaVenDesigns, a professional organization business for custom organization systems in clients homes/office spaces. Nyla strives to showcase her knowledge of budgeting, organization, and time-management skills to successfully fulfill the goals of her clients.*
www.nylavendesigns.com

Over 1,800 new women-owned businesses are created each day in the U.S.

Question for Contemplation:
Do you have another business you could create?

Pro Tip:
Find a business buddy. Find another woman business owner and commit to mutually supporting one another.

ELEVEN
WHY DO BUSINESS IF YOU DON'T LIKE IT?

SHERRI MATHENEY

"Be vulnerable, be yourself, and be proud to share your business wins and downfalls."

When I walked into my first Girl Boss meeting I felt nervous, excited and curious. I joined when there were only 100 members in the group. I walked in and was immediately greeted with smiles and ladies introducing themselves to me as if they had known me for years. My guard was instantly down and I knew in my heart I was in the right place. We sat at tables together and shared what our business was and our names. I didn't even officially have a business name.

However, I had been working on my business for a decade already. At that time, my confidence was pretty low and I was not sure I wanted to continue working in the insurance industry even though I was good at it I lacked the business mindset portion of it. I remember getting asked about my business and I said I do insurance but I'm not sure I want to. I was instantly called out by Jamie, who said, "Why are you even here if you don't like your business?" Her comment stuck with me. I began to change my mindsetinstantly, and went home to come up with a name for mybusiness.

I started my business 12 years ago. I was a bartender and someone who sat at my bar said you should get into the health insurance industry, you'd be good at it. I was always looking for something else I could do for a career. As much as I loved bartending, it wasn't going to be sustainable long term with a small child at home. I always loved helping people and I knew this was a career I could do without having a 4 year degree. I got licensed immediately and worked insurance during the day and was a bartender at night. It was scary going into a commission only field and not knowing what I was doing. Eventually I was able to make insurance my full time career. I jumped for joy the day I was able to quit my bartending job.

I was first invited to Girl Boss by Alyssa VanNuys. I actually hired her to organize my house. We got to talking about both of our businesses and the next day I got an invite to the Facebook group. When I went to my first meeting I did not know what to expect. I walked in and was greeted with smiles and it seemed like everyone was so excited to be there. I didn't realize it at the time, but my business lacked professionalism and purpose. I was stuck in the repetitive nature of calling "leads" and just signing people up. I quickly learned I was not working my business properly. I lacked passion and enthusiasm for what I was doing. I didn't have professional pictures, a logo or a website.

SPGB completely changed how I view my business. One of the first events we did was a headshot event where I was able to get my first ever professional photos taken. I was able to get a website made, a professional Facebook page and a logo. I learned there's a lot more that goes into a business than I thought. I felt so good and I now looked and sounded professional. I have learned so much about marketing and what to put on social media. After about a year in Girl Boss, working on my business and going to every meeting I could, I started to get calls from the girls needing help, which soon snowballed into the girls referring me to other people needing help. Before I knew it my phone was and still is ringing several times a day. I feel amazing being a part of this awesome, supportive community of women. Girl Boss opened my eyes to networking in general. I always had this idea that networking was scary and stuffy. It's anything but that! I've made so many friends, connections, learned about business and how I could improve my business.

My advice to anyone on the fence about SPGB or networking in general is just do it. I go to meetings to make friends and learn and it happens to help my business blossom as well. Listen to advice given and learn from it. Go to every meeting you can and just dig into the greatness that happens every week. Be vulnerable, be yourself, and be proud to share your business wins and downfalls.

Sherri Matheney *has been a dedicated Florida health insurance agent for 12 years. She is licensed in 33 states and has worked with clients in over 25 states. www.healthinsurancewithsherri.com.*

Only 7% of Fortune 500 CEOs are women.

Question for Contemplation:
Are you comfortable in leadership roles? If yes, how can you stand out as a leader? If not, what stands in your way?

Pro Tip:
Leadership becomes essential as your company grows. You are bound to need assistance! Delegation is key to scaling: recognize that you can't do everything yourself, and surround yourself with talented people.

Be sure to be inclusive and consider other perspectives.

Always invite others to contribute their ideas, and be sure to clearly and consistently communicate goals to your team so they understand what may affect them.

TWELVE
FINDING MY MOJO COMMUNITY

AMY JUNE (AJ) WIGGINS

"My very first meeting was nothing short of magical!"

WHEN I FIRST MOVED TO FLORIDA, I WAS TRAVELING around town to town as a mobile personal trainer. The driving was monotonous and I soon found myself looking for another way. A friend from back in Chicago recommended I join a women's networking group. Thinking about all the new friendships I would make, I decided to go to my first meeting. I enjoyed the women that I had met in Clearwater and decided to join the group because of the tremendous welcome from the Fort Myers and Cape Coral chapter meetings. Since this group was virtual, I was enjoying meeting new women from all across the United States. After many months, however, I discovered that much of the support that I had was turning into long conversations of gossip and criticism of the other women bosses. It was becoming "cliquey" and I couldn't trust whether they were talking behind my back or promoting me so I detached from the group completely.

While I was trying to decide my next way to meet new people in this new land, I was told by a couple different individuals who knew nothing of each other, the same thing: you belong in St. Pete. They told me my personality and all the things I stood for resonated with the people in St. Petersburg. I wondered how a city could attract a certain kind of person, someone like myself. I took a chance and looked on Indeed for a personal trainer position and found one that particularly appealed to the entrepreneur and was an actual space I could have clients come to. I discussed it with my husband and he knew this was the thing I had been sending out to the universe to receive. Having a virtual business while looking for new clients in the area was helpful, but I needed to find a way to get out into the community, so I started teaching stroller fitness classes and learned from Christie, a St. Pete Girl Boss, how to get everything running and what groups to advertise in. She was an amazing resource to me as a newbie and a tremendous support to so many non-profits in the community and the St. Pete Chamber of Commerce.

As part of the St. Pete Girl Boss Facebook Group, I found an opportunity that created wellness expert services as a part of a collaborative gift package. The Entrepreneur Wellness Project was formed and my offer was a stress-busting kickboxing class for bosses to get their work aggressions out in a healthy way. Elaine of Expert Color Solutions bought her friend, Dana, a gift package. Dana loved the class so much that she got Elaine, and their friend Anne to join. These women when put together can get my face muscles hurting from all the laughing we do. Since the original three we have added five more women and are growing strong.

These women are truly the most supportive, non-judgemental women I have ever had the pleasure of knowing.

I started training at this open-air facility in St. Pete in September 2022.

In addition to my classes I had a handful of personal training clients that I was seeing 2-3 times a week. May was coming to a close and some of my older clients were having a hard time exercising in the heat. I noticed a post in the St. Pete Girl Boss group that was asking if any trainers needed a space to rent. I spoke with the manager, Jen, also a Girl Boss, and loved the model that they outlined. I quickly set up a meeting to come see the facility and fell instantly in love with the atmosphere. I knew my clients would love the air conditioning, so I made the switch in June 2023. Moving to this new space at Best Day Fitness allowed me to double my income from the previous year. It wasn't until after I had been there for a month that Jen convinced me to go to my first St. Pete Girl Boss meeting on a Friday morning

My very first meeting was nothing short of magical! The energy in the bright room, the welcoming smiling faces, and the segment on wins had me feeling on top of the world. Since that first meeting I have become a VIP Uplevel Member and coordinated FitBoss, a free fitness class weekly for uplevel members. I am amazed by how large the group has become since I first joined and I always enjoy meeting new faces and finding ways to collaborate with others in order to bring the best to the people of St. Pete.

When the universe told me to move to Florida, I had no idea the tremendous growth that I would undergo. I had no idea the types of deep friendships I would make. I had no idea the kind of boss that I would become. I had no idea what this city would help me create for so many people, but I took a chance and I am infinitely grateful because I am sincerely the happiest I have ever been. I have many plans for empowering more individuals to create a happier, healthier life through exercise and couldn't think of a better place to do it than with my friendly entrepreneurs at the St. Pete Girl Bosses and the magnificent city of St. Petersburg.

Amy (AJ) Wiggins *is a wife and mom of two intelligent girls. She is the owner of AJ's Personal Training and is a former physical and health educator that loves nature and empowering others.*
www.ajspersonaltraining.com

Women-led startups deliver 35% higher return on investment than male-led firms.

Question for Contemplation:
Do you think there is an innate difference in how women lead businesses?

Pro Tip:
Spend some time discussing leadership with women you know. Consider a book club from strong women leaders.

You'll notice that the characteristics of females in charge are not necessarily aggressive, but more aligned with feminine energy.

Work to be intentional about using those skills and characteristics when you have the opportunity.

THIRTEEN
RECLAIMING MY VOICE

GRACE LAGER

"It's about healing, reclaiming power, and dismantling the patriarchy one voice at a time."

"Want to meet me there Friday? I'm speaking, and I'd love your support."

Those words got me in the door—into a world I wasn't sure I belonged to. Me? A businesswoman? Doubt clouded my thoughts. I had already experienced a failed business. I was an academic, after all. Could I make this new venture work?

When my friend invited me to join her at the St. Pete Girl Boss Friday Coffee, I agreed, more out of a desire to support her than any real belief in my place there. As a mom of two with twenty years in academia, I wasn't sure I belonged among women who looked polished, confident, and, well, legitimate. But deep down, I knew I had to be there—not just for her, but for me. I was determined to prove the naysayers and doubters wrong this time.

I arrived a few minutes before 9 a.m. I was filled with excitement about the beautiful space and the new possibilities that awaited. As soon as I stepped inside, the excitement I felt vanished. Imposter syndrome hit me like a tidal wave. These women—and there had to be at least a hundred of them—exuded confidence, success, and purpose. What was I doing here?

I found a seat at a table in the back, filled with strangers. One woman commented on our similar curly hair and pulled out a chair for me. The gesture felt kind, but my defenses were up. Was she genuine? Or was she trying to sell me something?

And then, everything shifted. The energy in the room exploded as Barbra Barker took the stage. Her electric presence and the unbridled support among the women in the room woke something in me. I was drawn into the spirit of what it meant to be a girl boss. The high energy, the solidarity, the genuine joy of women supporting women—it started to chip away at my doubts. When the main speaker took the stage, her confidence, humor, and insight resonated deeply with me. I was hooked. I knew I would be back.

Before my first SPGB meeting, I had just begun coming to terms with childhood trauma I had suppressed for years. This discovery shocked me. How had I ignored something so significant for so long? It hit me then—my entire life, I had been silenced. As a child, as a student, as a young career woman.

I wasn't alone. This silencing, this marginalization, is something many women experience. The specifics may differ, but the message society sends women is consistent: Be quiet. Stay small. Stay in your lane.

Starting my business was my way of reclaiming my voice, both literally and metaphorically. But it wasn't just about me. It was about empowering other women to do the same. St. Pete Girl Boss illuminated the brilliance that women bring to the world—a brilliance that is so often minimized or dismissed because of cultural norms. Being in a room filled with women who were also healing, who were also scared to raise their voices, who were also doubting their worth, brought me strength. I realized I had found my sisters.

My business is about more than just building confidence or teaching public speaking. It's about healing, reclaiming power, and dismantling the patriarchy one voice at a time.

For twenty years, I worked in academia and nonprofit sectors. I had imagined a different career, one that celebrated innovation and fresh ideas. Instead, I found myself constrained by rigid hierarchies. Despite being asked to apply for promotions and long-term contracts, I was continually rejected. Socially isolated in my department, I felt marginalized and unseen.

I was trying to break the mold, but every effort was met with rejection. I wasn't allowed to innovate or create new programs that could benefit both the college and myself. Instead, I was boxed in—called upon to take on extra work for little or no pay, while the recognition and opportunities went elsewhere.

I felt invisible, disillusioned, and on the verge of burnout. I knew I couldn't stay on this path. I couldn't spend the rest of my life feeling unwanted, undervalued, and fearful of losing my job year after year.

Despite my failed business, I decided to try again, this

time determined to take a different approach. St. Pete Girl Boss entered my life at just the right time, providing a community of like-minded women who were not only focused on their own success but were committed to lifting other women with them; these were my people; this was my space.

Since joining SPGB, my mindset has completely shifted. Instead of fear and isolation, I am fearless and supported. Collaboration with other women entrepreneurs has become my lifeblood. Every partnership, every happy hour, every Facebook group interaction has built my confidence and expanded my network in ways I never imagined.

The women I've met through SPGB have become more than colleagues, they are my friends, collaborators, and inspiration. They've helped me see my worth, not just as an entrepreneur but as a person. The validation I once sought in academia is now coming from this supportive community.

What's even more powerful is that this transformation has bled into my other roles. I bring the lessons I've learned as a Girl Boss into the classroom, teaching my students about the importance of collaboration, confidence, and community.

SPGB has empowered me to take control of my destiny. I feel motivated, supported, and driven to push forward for myself and every woman who has ever doubted her voice. To every woman on this journey: embrace your nerves, and don't let self-doubt hold you back. You don't have to go it alone. Reach out, find your community, and lean on them when the road gets tough. Collaboration is your superpower. Use it.

Grace Lager, PhD, *is a leading expert in communication strategies for women, combining over two decades of academic and real-world experience. As the founder of The Speaker Spark, she helps high-achieving women find their voices. Grace is a also a college professor, mother of two, and holds a Myers-Briggs Type Indicator certification. www.TheSpeakerSpark.com*

Just under half of all female founders believe a lack of available mentors or advisers holds them back.

Question for Contemplation:
How can you support other women who are learning what you already know?

Pro Tip:
Volunteer for your local SCORE chapter or chamber of commerce and offer to teach women's classes around a favorite business topic.

FOURTEEN
THE STRENGTH OF VULNERABILITY

CARMEN ESCOBAR

"The world as we know it wasn't designed with us, as women, in mind. But that doesn't mean it can't change. I believe it's time we start designing the world we want to live in—one where we can feel confident and free to talk about our nature without shame or judgment."

I STILL VIVIDLY REMEMBER MY FIRST TUESDAY COFFEE, invited by Jamie Anderson from Weapon Brand, my first collaboration. Excitement and nervousness washed over me in equal measure. Though I had been a member of the St. Pete Girl Bosses (SPGB) group for a while, the thought of actually showing up in person had always terrified me.

Walking into that room, I was overwhelmed by the energy of women who fully believed in themselves. They were fearless, stepping out of their comfort zones, showing up as boldly as they could, and—most strikingly—supporting each other. It was a new experience for me. My past interactions with women had often felt competitive, with each person planting their flag and defending their space. I was used to the idea that you needed to claim your ground early, or risk being trampled by someone else.

At the time, I had plenty of reasons to keep to myself. I was grieving the loss of my mother and navigating life felt overwhelming. I wasn't interested in anyone else's world—I barely understood my own. Isolating myself seemed like the best defense. My social flag read "LEAVE ME ALONE," and I waved it high. I felt like my social skills had vanished, never to return.

But when God has a plan for you, the universe conspires to make it happen. As much as I wanted to remain hidden, there was no escaping the path laid out for me. Despite my resistance, I knew I had been given talents and dreams too big to ignore, even though I often felt unworthy of them. Deep down, I knew I belonged somewhere.

The turning point came when I walked into that Tuesday Coffee. As I stood among these women, listening to their stories and seeing their smiles, something stirred inside me. I wanted to tell my story, too. Yet, when Sandy asked me to introduce myself, I froze. The words wouldn't come, and all I could manage was, "I'm not ready." She moved on, but not before assuring me, with warmth in her voice, "When you are ready, we'll be here for you."

Well, I'm ready now.

I discovered my "why" after quitting my last job due to health reasons. In 2018, I was diagnosed with PMDD (Premenstrual Dysphoric Disorder), and my life since has been a healing journey—one that felt like a never-ending waxing treatment for the soul, except no one was counting to three.

The challenges and judgments I faced along the way often felt unbearable, and there were times I doubted my strength to handle it all.

One of the hardest aspects was having to explain how my health was intricately tied to my menstrual cycle. Discussing something so personal and, frankly, uncomfortable in a professional environment was an experience I wouldn't wish on anyone. It made me realize that this wasn't how work should feel. No one should have to defend their health in the workplace, especially over something so deeply tied to their biology. I reached a breaking point where I had to make a choice: my health or my job. So, I chose me. I jumped. I quit.

At that moment, I made a promise to myself: I would work hard to create a path for the next woman who faced a similar struggle. The world as we know it wasn't designed with us, as women, in mind. But that doesn't mean it can't change. I believe it's time we start designing the world we want to live in—one where we can feel confident and free to talk about our nature without shame or judgment.

The heart of my business is rooted in this vision. I'm deeply connected to the idea of creating a safe space for women to grow, prosper, and most importantly, express themselves without fear of judgment. Too often, we feel lost under the weight of our passions and aspirations, uncertain if we can truly hold the world in our hands. But we can.

I got tired of feeling confined by those limitations, and I want you to get tired too. I want you to get tired of staying where you are and make a change for yourself. That's my why. I want to be the "bad influence" they warned you about —the one who inspires you to be bold, be fearless, and take a chance on yourself. Because baby, time isn't coming back.

Before becoming more actively involved with St. Pete Girl Bosses (SPGB), I had already been a member of the group since its inception, but my lack of self-confidence held me back from fully participating. Despite this, I still connected with other girl bosses in the Facebook group. I considered myself a "lone wolf"—someone who preferred to work in isolation, believing I could thrive without much outside influence. At least, that's what I told myself.

A year after joining SPGB, I graduated with a degree in Media & Communications, feeling ready to take on the world. I was eager to make my mark, but I quickly realized that navigating the business world with women was an entirely different experience from working with men. To succeed, I needed to tap into a different part of myself—a feminine side I hadn't fully acknowledged.

This was a challenge for me. As an introvert, I cherished my solitude and quiet moments. However, there was something magnetic about being in a room full of women who were not only ambitious but also supportive of each other's dreams. Each meeting I attended introduced me to a new story of triumph, a fresh opportunity, or a collective win. It was inspiring, but also intimidating.

I wasn't ready for that level of openness and camaraderie. In the environment I came from, you didn't share your successes for fear of envy. I believed that if I shared my dreams, someone might steal them, and that belief kept me guarded. I was used to blaming external circumstances for my failures rather than taking responsibility for my own habits and actions.

My perspective began to shift after attending my first BFD (Big Friggin' Deal) meeting. The energy was electric, unlike anything I had experienced before. I remember sitting

THE STRENGTH OF VULNERABILITY

at a Tuesday Coffee, preparing to listen to the speakers and follow the usual networking schedule, when suddenly, the room erupted into music. It felt like the start of a Tony Robbins seminar, full of energy and excitement.

After joining St. Pete Girl Bosses (SPGB), my life and business underwent a transformation I never saw coming. At first, I was hesitant—afraid, even—to share my story. I felt damaged, broken, and unworthy of being anything more than just another business owner looking for clients. I didn't think my voice mattered, so I kept it quiet. But over time, something shifted. I found myself not only telling my story but standing in front of other women as a speaker—twice. The change was profound, and it left me wondering why I hadn't believed in the power of femininity and community sooner.

My fear of speaking has transformed into a hunger for connection. Now, instead of avoiding the spotlight, I seek out opportunities to ask questions, to learn more about other women's businesses, their stories, and their struggles. Where I once wanted only to be brave, I now feel as though I've found that bravery. And it's not the loud, aggressive kind, but a quiet, steady courage that comes from knowing you belong. I've realized that strength is not found in going it alone, but in standing alongside others and embracing the power of community.

The most important lesson I've learned is that we are never truly alone. Our pain, our experiences, and even our healing—these are all things we share, whether we realize it or not. Meeting so many remarkable women in SPGB has shown me that vulnerability is not weakness, but the ultimate act of courage. Asking for help, admitting you don't have all the answers, and leaning on others during difficult times—these are the moments that define true bravery.

Since giving myself the grace to be imperfect, I've gained a new sense of freedom. Perfection no longer feels like a requirement for success; instead, authenticity has become my guiding principle. My business mindset has shifted from trying to "do it all" to understanding that collaboration and support are vital for growth. And in that shift, I have found a sense of peace. I no longer fear telling my story—I celebrate it.

Words of wisdom: If there's one thing I've learned, it's that vulnerability is your greatest strength. Don't be afraid to share your story—your challenges, your failures, and your triumphs. The more you open up, the more you realize that you're not alone in your journey. Ask for help when you need it, and never feel ashamed for not having all the answers. Remember, perfection isn't the goal—progress is. Surround yourself with women who lift you up, and don't hesitate to be that source of encouragement for others. Bravery isn't the absence of fear; it's showing up despite it.

Carmen Escobar *is a Creative Designer, a mother of two, and a USAF Vet Spouse, Notary Public and a member of the American Translators Association (ATA). Through her design agency, Kustomee Brands, she excels in developing and implementing creative and strategic marketing initiatives.*

Businesses owned by Black women earn significantly less than businesses run by other women.

Question for Contemplation:
Why do you think Black owned businesses earn less? How can you help distribute resources across diverse business owners in your community?

Pro Tip:
Highlight the voices and experiences of successful Black-owned businesses by following them on social media and sharing their content. Create networking experiences that include a variety of ethnicities and viewpoints in order to better support mentorship and resources across your community.

FIFTEEN
THE MAGIC OF COLLABORATION: UNLEASHING THE GIRL BOSS EFFECT

NICOLE SAUNCHES

"In the St Pete Girl Boss Networking Group, we've already seen the power of collaboration and the incredible things we can achieve when we work together. The investment cooperative is a natural extension of this spirit, offering a tangible way for us to make a lasting impact on our community."

IN THE HEART OF ST. PETERSBURG, A QUIET REVOLUTION is unfolding—a movement driven by women who understand that true power lies not just in individual success, but in the collective strength of collaboration. The St Pete Girl Boss Networking Group is more than just a gathering of entrepreneurs; it's a thriving ecosystem where ideas are nurtured, dreams are fueled, and success is shared.

NICOLE SAUNCHES

The Birth of the Girl Boss Effect

The "girl boss" phenomenon is more than a trendy term—it's a declaration of independence, resilience, and ambition. It's the spirit of women who refuse to be confined by traditional roles and instead carve their paths with determination and grace. But within the St Pete Girl Boss community, this effect is amplified by one core belief: we are stronger together.

From the moment I attended my first meeting, I knew that St Pete Girl Boss was different, special, and magical. Unlike the stuffy, transaction-focused networking where I left feeling depleted energetically this group felt like home. The energy was palpable, filled with genuine connections and a shared purpose. I didn't just find a networking group that day; I found my community.

In the early days of the St Pete Girl Boss Networking Group, members came together with a shared vision—to uplift and support one another in their entrepreneurial journeys. The magic began when these women realized that their individual goals could be better achieved through collaboration rather than competition.

The Power of Collaboration

Collaboration is the cornerstone of the St Pete Girl Boss movement. It's about pooling resources, sharing knowledge, and leveraging each other's strengths to achieve more than any one person could alone. In this community, collaboration isn't just encouraged; it's celebrated. Take, for example, an event that perfectly encapsulates the spirit of collaboration within our group. I attended Brenda Shadday's opening of Bronze Fox Beauty at her new location, where I had the pleasure of mingling with fellow Girl Bosses and providing products for her VIP giveaways, as well as a raffle item. The atmosphere was electric, filled with the energy of women supporting women.

In the midst of the event, I had to step away for a real estate showing. As I pulled up to the showing, I received a text message from fellow Girl Boss Kelly Abanda. She asked if she could share my information with someone she had just met at the event who was looking for a real estate agent. I thanked her for the referral and, of course, told her she could share my information. After the showing, I returned to Brenda's event, where I had the chance to meet Megan McIntyre, Kelly's referral, in person. Little did I know that this brief encounter would lead to something much more significant.

Fast forward 15 months, and I'm thrilled to say that I have closed four transactions with Megan and her family. Beyond the business, Megan and her family have become dear friends, a relationship that blossomed out of a simple act of connection and collaboration.

This is the power of collaboration. It's the realization that by joining forces, we can create something far greater than the sum of our parts. In the St Pete Girl Boss Networking Group, this philosophy is ingrained in everything we do. Whether it's co-hosting events, sharing platforms, or simply brainstorming over coffee, collaboration is the secret sauce that drives our success.

Addressing Affordability: A Vision for the Future

As the cost of living in St. Petersburg continues to rise, many residents find themselves grappling with the harsh realities of affordability. This issue has become especially pressing in the wake of rapid appreciation during the COVID years, which has further exacerbated the divide between those who can afford to live and thrive in our community and those who cannot. The challenges are even more pronounced for marginalized and disenfranchised communities, who have historically been affected by systemic oppression and institutionalized racism.

I envision the creation of an investment cooperative—a bold and innovative approach to ensuring that our community remains accessible and prosperous for all its members. This cooperative would offer group investment opportunities, allowing local residents to pool their resources, utilize tools such as the debt service coverage ratio mortgages, 1031 exchanges, and investment directly in the community, rather than watching outside investors, who may not have our community's best interests at heart, dominate the market.

Empowering Marginalized Communities Through Collective Investment

The concept of an investment cooperative is particularly vital for marginalized and disenfranchised communities. These communities have often been excluded from traditional investment opportunities due to systemic barriers, such as redlining, discriminatory lending practices, and economic disinvestment. These barriers have not only stifled economic growth within these communities but have also prevented individuals from building generational wealth.

The investment cooperative I propose would turn this narrative on its head. By allowing community members to invest collectively, we can democratize access to wealth-building opportunities and empower those who have been historically disenfranchised. This cooperative would prioritize projects that benefit the community as a whole, such as developing affordable housing, supporting local businesses, and revitalizing underinvested neighborhoods.

Imagine a scenario where members of the communities can buy into a cooperative that invests in the very neighborhoods where they live. Instead of being priced out or pushed out by gentrification, they become stakeholders in the development process. They have a say in what gets built, where it gets built, and how the profits are distributed. This model not only preserves the cultural and historical integrity of these neighborhoods but also ensures that the economic benefits are shared equitably among those who live there.

Utilizing the Power of the St Pete Girl Boss Network

The St Pete Girl Boss Network, with its diverse and talented membership, is uniquely positioned to support this investment cooperative. Our network is filled with women who are experts in various fields, from finance and law to marketing and construction. By leveraging the skills and resources within our group, we can ensure that the cooperative is not only successful but also sustainable in the long term.

For instance, financial experts within our network can help structure the cooperative in a way that maximizes returns for all members while minimizing risk. Legal professionals can ensure that the cooperative operates within a framework that protects the rights of all investors, particularly those from marginalized communities. Marketing strategists can craft campaigns that raise awareness about the cooperative and attract a broad base of support. And local contractors and designers can be engaged to manage renovations and development projects, ensuring that they reflect the needs and values of the community.

A New Model for Community-Driven Development

The investment cooperative represents a new model for community-driven development—one that puts power back into the hands of the people. It's a model that challenges the status quo and offers a path forward for those who have been left behind by traditional economic systems. By fostering a sense of ownership and agency, the cooperative empowers individuals to take control of their financial futures and contribute to the well-being of their community.

This cooperative isn't just about making money; it's about making a difference. It's about creating opportunities for those who have been systematically excluded from wealth-building and ensuring that the benefits of economic development are shared equitably. It's about building a stronger, more resilient community where everyone has a stake in the future.

Beyond the Financial: Building Social Capital

In addition to financial empowerment, the investment cooperative also has the potential to build social capital within marginalized communities. Social capital refers to the networks of relationships and trust that facilitate cooperation and collective action. In many disenfranchised communities, social capital has been eroded by decades of disinvestment and neglect. The cooperative can help rebuild these networks by bringing people together around a shared purpose. By participating in the cooperative, members not only gain access to financial opportunities but also become part of a supportive community. They forge connections with other investors, collaborate on projects, and build relationships based on mutual trust and respect. This social capital can be just as valuable as the financial returns, as it strengthens the fabric of the community and fosters a sense of belonging and solidarity.

The Future of the Investment Cooperative

As we look to the future, the potential of the investment cooperative is limitless. It can serve as a model for other communities facing similar challenges, demonstrating that collective action can overcome even the most entrenched barriers. It can inspire other marginalized communities to take control of their economic destinies and build a future that reflects their values and aspirations.

In the St Pete Girl Boss Networking Group, we've already seen the power of collaboration and the incredible things we can achieve when we work together. The investment cooperative is a natural extension of this spirit, offering a tangible way for us to make a lasting impact on our community. By embracing this vision, we can create a brighter, more inclusive future for St. Petersburg—one where everyone has the opportunity to thrive.

A Passion for Transforming Healthcare

Beyond the investment cooperative, another passion of mine lies in transforming the healthcare system. My journey into functional medicine profoundly changed my life, leading me to embrace a holistic approach to wellness that prioritizes proactive, natural solutions. Now, I am committed to sharing this approach with others by serving as a consultant for wellness-minded health professionals.

My mission is clear: to transform our healthcare system one patient and one practice at a time. I work with health professionals who are eager to integrate customized, natural solutions that deliver better patient outcomes. This mission is deeply personal, rooted in my own health transformation, and I believe it's time to bring this holistic, functional medicine approach into the mainstream.

As part of this mission, I see endless possibilities for collaboration within the St Pete Girl Boss Network. The wealth of knowledge, creativity, and innovation within this community is immense, and together, we can revolutionize how healthcare is delivered. Whether it's through partnerships with local wellness practitioners, creating educational content, or developing new wellness products, the potential for impact is vast.

Creating a Collaborative Culture

So how can we, as female entrepreneurs, foster a culture of collaboration in our own circles? It starts with a mindset shift—from competition to cooperation. Here are a few principles that have guided the St Pete Girl Boss Networking Group:

1. Open Communication: Collaboration thrives in an environment where ideas can be freely exchanged. Be open to sharing your vision and listening to others.

2. Celebrate Success Together: When one of us wins, we all win. Celebrate the achievements of your peers as if they were your own.

3. Leverage Diverse Strengths: Each of us brings unique skills to the table. Recognize and appreciate the diversity of talents within your network.

4. Be Generous with Support: Offer your expertise, time, or resources without expecting immediate returns. The more you give, the more you'll receive in the long run.

5. Stay Connected: Regularly engage with your network. Collaboration isn't a one-time event—it's an ongoing process that requires continuous nurturing.

The Future of Girl Boss Collaboration

As the St Pete Girl Boss Networking Group continues to grow, so too does the potential for groundbreaking collaborations. The future is bright, not just for individual entrepreneurs, but for the collective impact we can make together. In a world that often pits women against each other, this group stands as a shining example of what's possible when we choose to lift each other up.

Imagine what we can achieve when we all embrace the girl boss effect and harness the power of collaboration. Together, we can redefine what it means to be successful, not just in business, but in life. This is the magic of the St Pete Girl Boss movement—a magic that we create, together.

Nicole Saunches *is a real estate advisor with Coastal Properties Group International, an exclusive member of Forbes Global Properties. She is also host of the Selling St. Pete podcast.*
www.sellingstpetefl.com

CONCLUSIONS IN REFLECTION

ANGELA YARBER

Are you feeling inspired? Empowered? Emboldened?

I know I am.

And here's the secret. These essays, written vulnerably and powerfully by a handful of girl bosses, are only a small glimpse at the transformative power of an intentional women's networking community to create change in the world. There are thousands of other women thriving because of SPGB.

Is the SPGB founder, Sandy Bean, magical and brilliant? Yes, absolutely. Are these essayists? You betcha. But so are you. So are women committed to making substantive change in the world with our businesses, women dismantling the patriarchy one entrepreneurial journey at a time. Whether it's confronting the nagging imposter syndrome sitting on your shoulder, collaborating with like-minded women, or finding a girl boss who can coach you through using Quickbooks without talking to you like you're a complete fool, intentional women's networking groups are dismantling unjust systems through the transformative power of community.

Angie Williams reminded us that an inclusive women's networking community, combined with a pretty epic alter ego, can pull you from the depths of depression and help you grapple with grief, while simultaneously building your business. Stacey Halbert discussed the freedom of autonomy in entrepreneurship and how SPGB showed her that "the sky's the limit." Kamysha Martin's essay emboldened us to live unabashedly into our multi-hyphenate selves rather than limiting our entrepreneurship to one thing alone. Hailey Rank wrote with vulnerability and joy about how an intentional women's networking community not only improved her business, but helped her survive her spouse's gut-wrenching time in the hospital. Lisa Alban discussed the ways mindset shifts created transformational change in her life and business. Melania Mersades talked about the power of being truly seen in a community, as a healer, as a businesswoman, as a Latina girl boss. Lisa Ann Marone wrote about the all-too-familiar feeling of imposter syndrome and how a women's networking community gave her confidence and peace. Late in Life Lesbian Life Coach, Kathy Houston, reminded us that the secret sauce of a women's networking group is the safety of community.

Allyson Mixon illustrated that our ability to network has the power to shape our net worth. Nyla Williams showed how your past—even with an ACE score of 10—doesn't have to define your future, especially when you have the transformative power of collaboration with other girl bosses. Sherri Matheney's essay illustrated the power of professionalism, vulnerability, and sharing your wins in community. AJ Wiggins reminded readers that finding your community may just double your income. Grace Lager's story of transitioning from academic to entrepreneur within a women's networking community empowered you to dismantle the patriarchy one voice at a time. Carmen Escobar wrote of the transformative power of community and vulnerability in creating, not simply a business, but a new world. And Nicole Saunches took us from past and present with a vision for the future grounded in the girl boss effect.

Whether it's inspirational essays, the statistics that back them up, questions for contemplation, or practical tips, Sandy and I hope this book has galvanized you to take the next steps in expanding and deepening your business. In fact, I want to offer one more practical tip that stems from my own work and wisdom: publishing.

I believe there is no greater outlet for sharing your message—and the message of your business—than through publishing. In my estimation, it is your greatest marketing tool and an incontrovertible method for establishing your expertise. In short, publishing a book (or even an essay to start) is the key to launching your business and brand into the stratosphere. This is what it means to live what I call the dream authorpreneur life.

Author + Entrepreneur = Authorpreneur.

In my own book coaching and publishing company, and even in the development of this very anthology, I work with writers and entrepreneurs regarding how to create programs that align with the deep, abiding WHY behind your book so that these programs, combined with your writing, can fund your dream life. Interestingly, the community where I've done this the most is with clergy. And if you're automatically picturing a white male priest, clad in golden vestments standing at a storied pulpit, think again. I created a program called Ministry from the Margins Books which essentially gathers a cohort of queer, BIPOC, and women clergy together–the kind of spiritual leaders usually banned from and excluded by most churches–and empowers them in writing a book that makes a difference in the world and then leverages the book for living the authorpreneur life. Because ministers–and particularly marginalized ministers–are wildly undercompensated and overworked. Sound familiar, entrepreneur?

When I saw this authorpreneur approach work again and again with marginalized clergy, a light bulb went off in my mind. This same approach could work for another marginalized, overworked, and undercompensated group: women entrepreneurs.

You know all those statistics and stereotypes listed throughout this book? The stats reminding us that women earn less, but work more? The stereotypes that claim women don't have the right personalities for leadership? Again I say: Barf. Throw all that out the window because it does not belong in this revolutionary intentional community we are creating.

Instead, let's harness the energy of Diana, who told me after her book made it to #1 in three different categories in less than 24 hours of publication, "I'm living the life small child me dreamed about." Let's channel the wisdom of Kay who not only finally decided to double her prices after publishing her book, but ended up tripling her income in the process. Let's be like Terri, who left the toxic job that was slowly killing her for nearly 25 years because we used her book to create an "off ramp" from academia so she could live the creative life of a writer and artist.

You, too, have the power to live the authorpreneur life of

your dreams, dear entrepreneur. Because you have a message worth sharing, a business primed to change the world, and a powerful story behind WHY you started such a business. The girl bosses in this book have shared glimpses into their stories. What about you? Are you ready to share yours?

Launch your revolutionary business into the stratosphere by publishing a book for the global good! Learn how at www.tehomcenter.org

A RETURN TO THE FOUNDER: SANDY'S CONCLUSION

SANDY BEAN

So how did you enjoy spending time with some Girl Bosses? As you lean into these women's stories, you are creating a future that is not shackled to the limiting past. I hope you are feeling inspired and connected to YOUR OWN magic. If you choose to do so (and I hope you do!), you are well on your way to building a community– small or large!-- to support the life you desire. Because the key to our success is more than individual action.

As you have seen, there is so much power within our relationships with our sisters.

The Harvard Center for International Development's 2024 Global Empowerment Meeting published a podcast titled "Why Investing in Women Benefits us All", which pointed out that "greater women's economic participation is important because women typically reinvest up to 90 percent of their earnings in their families and communities compared to only 30 to 40 percent among men. This in turn can help expedite development and overcome societal poverty." We can literally change the world with our success. And our success is deeply supported by connections with other women.

Ready to integrate more of your circle of women into your plan? Let's talk about practical steps. Here are three things you can actively cultivate with others that will support your enduring success. They are:

- Respect
- Visibility and Influence
- Resources, including money

Obtaining such things can be tricky. How do we heal from these situations that we did not create, but inherited? How do we become comfortable being seen and exercising our authority? How do we work with the women around us to build community that then creates good, both in our personal world and in the greater one?

Here are some ideas for things you can do within your existing network to get you started.

Collaborative Success Ingredient #1: Cultivating Respect

You might be thinking that you do respect yourself, but do you fully care for your needs, set boundaries, and feel aligned with the energy of the people and places you frequent? If not, there might be some work to do. First, we have to deeply respect ourselves, and there can be a substantial self-worth and self-respect deficit simply from growing up female with no other factors. Once you get there, you will notice the opportunities and folks coming toward you are higher quality. Healing, knowing what you want, and acting accordingly are essential for both self and outward respect.

A RETURN TO THE FOUNDER: SANDY'S CONCLUSION

Without respect, you will not allow yourself to build the success you desire.

Here are some things that have worked for me and other Girl Bosses.

First: Take ownership of your healing.

- If you notice that you are very hard on yourself, have trouble resting, setting boundaries, or feel like you need to do it all and then some, or if you have trouble asking for help, I ask that you begin to observe those patterns and take some space to address them. This may be a big ask if you have lots of other pieces to address, but make no mistake that feminine people are affected by that factor on top of anything else.
- If you notice jealousy cropping up when you meet a woman who has something you want, ask yourself why you feel that way. What is it waking up in you that presents an opportunity for reflection? Can you ask her for advice? Can you create a collaboration or a mentoring relationship rather than drive a wedge? Create alliances for healing collaboratively. Not everyone will be for you, but that does not mean someone is against you, either.
- Be the woman who spreads "good gossip." Heal the words in the world by speaking well of your sisters when they aren't around. This open energy creates magnetism that attracts your crew to you. Being impeccable with your word, as the book the *Four Agreements* suggests, puts the

message of respect into the world, and it's a reciprocal universe, friends.
- Extend that same love to self-talk.

Once you are on that path, I ask you to be authentic.

- We can be very self-conscious around other women. We must practice authenticity and vulnerability. Spend time understanding your desires so you can hear your own intuition.
- Understand that the way you do YOUR thing is not like anyone else. Think about all of the good Italian restaurants. There are so many! Can you choose a favorite song? Or a favorite book? Chances are, not really. But they are all Italian restaurants and songs and books. Think of your magic that way. Yes, maybe you're one of a million financial advisors, but you are the only one who does it the way you do it. By sinking into that through self-exploration, knowing your most beloved, ideal client, and being open about your strengths and purpose, you will attract the opportunities meant uniquely for you, and can add to teams and partnerships in your own way.
- The collaborative piece here is allowing those who care about you to help you witness this part of you. Honest conversations with women around you can often shed some light on your purpose or path in ways self-reflection cannot.
- On that note, say no to things that aren't right for you. Speak up when things don't seem just.

A RETURN TO THE FOUNDER: SANDY'S CONCLUSION

When you know you have women at your back, it becomes a little easier.

Collaborative Success Ingredient #2: Visibility

These next two principles of collaboration support ingredient two: visibility. Why does this matter? Because if you aren't keen on speaking up, promoting your business, meeting people, and being authentic, it is going to be hard for you not only to create community, but to market your business at all.

I know being seen can be pretty tricky for many of us. Imposter syndrome, invisible women syndrome, lack of confidence... there are lots of things we struggle with (and I do want to say that if you have a history of trauma, you may want to call in professional help). For some of us, being seen was actually dangerous at some point in our lives, so the vulnerability of showing up and letting others see us, literally and figuratively, may be tough.

Spending time with women who have been where you are now and are where you'd like to be is a wonderful way to support your comfort with visibility. It's much easier to be vulnerable in spaces where you feel safe and connected, and then you can go out into the wider world with more confidence! By creating space for compassion toward your negative feelings, imposter syndrome, and perceived inadequacy as part of a system into which you were born, we also create space for other women, and that becomes a relationship ripe with possibilities.

Try these things:

Learn from each other. There is something quite magical about the way you are seen when you are being mentored or mentoring someone else. This is the first step in creating larger visibility, is to allow yourself to receive and be seen. Learning from each other allows you to do that in a very constructive way.

- Collaborating is often about learning. Listen to listen, not to hear. Even those with less experience have different wisdom. Our internalized sexism has created an inherent bias against female knowledge. Seek out brilliant women who are willing to educate you, or mentor you. Offer that to others, if you are in a leadership role. This is a tremendous opportunity to create more space for diverse viewpoints and voices.
- It is okay to invest in coaches and courses, too. Pay ladies for things you want and need.

Elevate your own and each other's voices. This is where larger visibility comes in, especially for those of you who are pretty comfortable being seen. I am a huge proponent of building social capital and of sharing the messages and wisdom of women and creators of color as part of my platform.

- If you are a leader, use that to showcase others. Share your own experiences and knowledge unapologetically. Take other women seriously,

too. Reiterate their point if someone else talks over them or takes credit. This can happen both online and in person. This is a whole masterclass in and of itself, social capital, but basically, don't be afraid to show yourself and take other women with you.
- Bring up the names of your sisters when opportunities arise that would suit them. Connect, connect, connect. If you have witnessed someone's genius, take it upon yourself to create visibility for them when they are not around.
- And hire your connections, too– if you love them, use them for what you require and review and refer. Support women and black-women owned businesses.

Success Ingredient #3: Building Resources (money and power)

Truthfully, the other two ingredients should get you tuned into making more money in your business. Further, we create more access to resources and make more money when we put our efforts together, and not just by buying from each other. In fact, don't go into your connections necessarily expecting they are your target market. We can reach a larger audience with the products or services that we represent when our network of supporters knows what we do and respects us, so always be relationship-focused. This is more sustainable and will work longer term than selling to everyone you meet.

Here's something else I love for creating more business. Borrow each other's audiences!

Create mutually beneficial collaborations for business. This is a practical strategy that you can have a lot of fun with!

The keys to successful business collabs are as follows:

- You should all serve the same or similar audience.
- Think about all of the roles you play and how that figures into what you do and why you do it.
- Have clear expectations ahead of time– getting it in writing makes everything smoother and provides a structure that meets everyone's needs.
- Find someone who you truly enjoy, believe in, and will feel comfortable being alongside.
- If you are the one with more influence, it's okay to teach about successful collabs if you've done them before. And, it's okay to simply uplift someone and have that be your benefit, because you believe in them.
- Similarly, if you are newer, gratitude and paying it forward later are always part of the process.
- Think outside the box! There are SO many ways to collaborate, whether it is an event, a gift box, booking a speaker, doing a giveaway, creating a version of something together... if you are not the creative thinking type at the moment, find someone in your atmosphere who is, and start vibing with them.

A RETURN TO THE FOUNDER: SANDY'S CONCLUSION

- Remember, collaboration is a long game. Customer journeys can take time, so plan for that.

I hope some of these strategies we employ in Girl Boss give you some ideas about how to leverage the women around you in ways that benefit everyone. We are partners in building what's better.

Now, if you want to create groups or meetups that actually gather women together, that takes a little more planning. But, as this book has shown you, it is well worth the effort! If you are ready to start your own community (and I teach women who are ready to do so!), here are five steps to getting started.

1. Have a clear set of values and a clear purpose. This will help you decide on the kind of rules and culture you'd like to support with your community, and will help you set forth what you'll be doing together and what is and is not acceptable. Sit down and really think this through. Why do you want to gather people? What do they need, and what do you need?
2. Remember that people gather for a common purpose, but they stay because of bonds. Create opportunities for individuals to connect with each other, rather than just receiving information. Women need time to get to know each other.
3. Have a structure and a way to communicate. It is very helpful to loosely decide on the structure of your meetings, with room for the conversation to

flow. This will help you facilitate and will create safety for your members who know what to expect! Create activities and content that are predictable but have value and engage individual voices. And communication is so important! Collect email addresses or have a group chat so you can share logistics, rules, and whatever else suits your purpose.

4. Be what you want to see. Lead by example. Participate the way you want others to participate; be vulnerable, connect, show up. And, conversely, be ready for challenging conversations with those who may not be a good fit for what you are building and need to be removed. It happens.

5. Be consistent and move toward your goals. Building community takes time. By aligning with values and a purpose, you will hopefully feel great about what you are building, and therefore, be more patient with the growth process. Keeping it small is okay too! You should have some goals in mind for your community so you can make decisions about moves when options come about.

The Girl Boss Effect came about because the female entrepreneurs in St Petersburg, Florida found value in the culture and purpose of our group, so they invest time, energy, and love into it. I try to match those efforts, and learn and grow along with them. Overall, we see tremendous personal and professional growth in our Bosses, as well as deep and enduring friendships. We have had tremendous growth, but even in a smaller group, you can easily hold space and mentor others for success. Just remember, the goal is to gather women together, peel away the layers that generations have laid at our feet, and recognize the value and contributions of each member.

There is so much strength in numbers. Humans are not meant to do it alone; there is a reason the saying "it takes a village" exists.

I hope you find your village, and I cannot wait to see the effect that your magic brings.

With love,

Sandy Bean
Founder of St Pete Girl Boss

ACKNOWLEDGMENTS

Sandy's Acknowledgements

Writing this book has been a dream realized. I am profoundly grateful to Angela for the momentum and structure to make it happen. I believe so deeply in this mission and love behind this story, and I appreciate that she saw fit to put it into writing. Her patience, creativity and expertise are always invaluable.

Next, I want to thank my oldest daughter Madison, the bravest person I know. Her journey and healing provided the impetus for my own, and so without her, none of this magic would exist. Maddie, I love you, Austin, Hayden and Onyx endlessly.

And of course, I must thank those who believe in St. Pete Girl Boss, and continue to show up to support this community. The experiences shared by these incredible women have not only inspired this book but also transformed lives. Your collective spirits are a constant source of love and motivation. I am forever thankful that you are in my ever-expanding circle.

And to you, dear reader, for picking up this book and joining all of us. I hope these pages inspire you as much as the stories within (and those that have yet to be told!) them have inspired me.

Thank you for wanting more, for seeking connection, and for believing in the power of feminist community.

Angela's Acknowledgements

It has been a gift to edit this book alongside the fabulous Sandy Bean. Sandy, thank you for creating the St. Pete Girl Boss community and for showing me what it means to apply an intersectional feminist ethic to business. Along these lines, I'm also grateful to my business coach, Dr. Katy Valetine, who encouraged me to get involved in women's networking communities.

I want to acknowledge the courage and vulnerability it took for the amazing girl bosses in this book to write their essays, many publishing for the first time. Thank you for trusting this process, for making change in the world, and for sharing your wisdom so that others can thrive, as well.

Thank you to the revolutionary community that is Tehom Center Publishing, a press publishing feminist and queer authors, with a commitment to elevate BIPOC writers. The authors I have the privilege of publishing, the editors, designers, coaches, and social media mavens I have the joy of working with fill me with hope and galvanize me to make a difference in the world. I'm glad this book can be even a small part of that.

For my beloved team, my brilliant wife, Elizabeth, and my keiki, thanks for your endless support.

And for all the readers who dare to make a difference in the world with change-making entrepreneurship, thank you for reading. Life and business don't have to remain grounded in white supremacist cisheteropatriarchy that hustles us into burnout. Reading this book means you're imagining a better world for yourself, your business, and for others. So, thank you.

www.ingramcontent.com/pod-product-compliance
Lightning Source LLC
Chambersburg PA
CBHW060505030426
42337CB00015B/1745